SYMBOL

Family
Backpacking
Adventures

Bennie van der Walt

1995

© Copyright 1995
Symbol Books, a division of
   J.P. van der Walt & Son (Pty) Ltd.
Set in 10 on 12 pt Palatino
Reproduction by Mandi Printers CC, Murrayfield, Pretoria
Printed by CTP Book Printers (Pty) Ltd, Parow
Jacket design: Paul Eder
First impression: 1995

ISBN 0 7993 2234 2

Contents

Contents

PREFACE

In this beautiful land of ours with its truly remarkable heritage of wilderness areas that are only now being opened in various parts of the country, we are in dire need of information about backpacking. There is an increasing demand for those who always have had the opportunity of exploring the wonders of the wide open spaces, to share these experiences with other sectors of the population of the country — and with our children and our children's children. It is in this context that the author, a concerned citizen and dedicated hiker, takes us to the open spaces and enables us to share the experience of backpacking with the family.

My acquaintance with the writer began more than five years ago when he was an unusual visitor who used to come and camp at our campsite. What was unusual about him was that he used to camp for an extended period, ranging from two to three weeks. It was not long before my colleagues and I came to realise that he was not only an avid hiker, he was also a writer. This exceptional book allows him to share his knowledge and experience of the open spaces with others. I know that this practical guide on hiking with the family is based on Bennie van der Walt's actual experiences. He has a special interest in nature and history, and both passions were the driving force that made him explore the wonders of our country's natural heritage. This he now shares with you.

This book is by no means merely a glossy addition to

your bookshelf or coffee table. Its purpose is to help new-comers to hiking. It is based on 19 years of experience of hiking in various parts of the country, of which the greater part has been in the Natal Drakensberg. I like its simple style and non-technical language which make the book easy reading for the widest readership. Bennie has, in writing books such as this, kept in mind those readers of our population who have not yet had the privilege of enjoying this type of outdoor recreation. Once you have read it, you will realise that this is a modestly priced book which will serve greatly to fill a gap in the literature of backpacking.

I have, with great pride, taken the opportunity of introducing this book to you, because it ties in so well with what Monica Holst and I are doing in the Bergville District area. For the past two years, we have been taking mixed groups into the Drakensberg for extended hiking trips. Through these excursions we are trying to teach people about outdoor recreation, and we hope to enhance the understanding of the real value of nature, especially among rural people.

In conclusion I hope that the book will be a useful guide to those who have dreamed about backpacking adventures for the family, or would like to undertake any other type of hiking holiday — but also to those who have already experienced the joy of hiking. I therefore take enormous pleasure in supporting the publication of this book, and hope that all sectors of our community will benefit from reading it.

Bhekisisa Z. Khoza,
Officer-in-charge,
Royal National Park,
Natal Parks Board, Private Bag X1669, BERGVILLE, 3350.

INTRODUCTION

Many people in South Africa regard hiking as the exclusive domain of young adults: people in their late teens and twenties or early thirties. There is a general impression that both younger and older people are excluded.

It is probably only people who have never hiked who believe this. A hiker can be anyone, from an infant to a greybeard!

This fact was confirmed some time ago when I visited the head office of the Appalachian Trail Conference at Harper's Ferry in the United States. Until then, the youngest person to have walked the whole Appalachian Trail of 3 200 kilometres was a nine-year-old girl. In the course of 1980 a six-year-old boy, Michael Cogswell, set a new record, as, accompanied by his parents, he walked the whole distance. The office of the Appalachian Trail Conference has a framed declaration in his own handwriting stating: *I hiked the whole A.T. with my mom and dad. The trail was nice. I got strong. I learned a lot. Started 4-1-80. Finished 12-22-80. Michael Cogswell. Age 6.*

This family started hiking in the south (at Springer Mountain in the state of Georgia) in the early spring of 1980. They hiked through fourteen states and four seasons before reaching the north (Mount Katahdin in the state of Maine) in the winter. Their average rate for the 3 200 kilometres (about 2 100 miles) was about 13 kilometres a day!

Nobody has been born on the Appalachian Trail, although a hiking mother gave birth to her child in a sleeping bag on an isolated beach in the state of Washington. The proud parents carried it to civilization the following day. This baby must hold the hiking record for its age!

Contrary to expectations the Appalachian Trail has

record-holders (called 2 000 milers) not only among children. Various octogenarians have covered the five million hiking strides, either in sections or in one go.

For women who may think that hiking is a strenuous undertaking suitable only for men, there are many enlightening examples. I have a book called *Hiking the Appalachian Trail* (two volumes, more than 2 000 pages) in which 48 hikers who have covered the whole of the Appalachian Trail describe their experiences in fascinating detail. Among them there are quite a number of women. Dorothy Laker, a young student, is not alone in her achievement of having walked the distance unaccompanied three times. Emma Gatewood (better known as Grandma Gatewood), a mother of eleven children, walked the entire trail at the age of sixty-eight, and then repeated the feat twice — the last time in her seventy-seventh year!

America, of course, is the land of records. You would expect people to compete in setting the fastest time over the route. The record for the 3 200 km is still 67 days. Is the poor man who did this to be admired or pitied?

In passing: It is no longer an exceptional feat to tackle the five million strides of the Appalachian Route with backpack and boots. At least 1 000 hikers tackled the entire route in 1981 — and probably annually since.

I apologise for presenting you with the hiking history of the USA, but little of our own hiking history has been recorded; and it will probably be quite some time before we have an uninterrupted hiking trail from Soutpansberg in the Northern Province to the Cedarberg in the Western Cape! However, the USA's hiking details prove that hiking — unlike most other forms of sports and recreation — is suitable for the whole family.

I also feel that at today's hectic living pace it is essential that families together should do as many as possible recreational activities as a group. Hiking offers a unique opportunity to strengthen family ties that have become vulnerable.

Hiking with your family holds its own particular joys. However, there are also problems and challenges associated with family hiking. This book attempts to help hiking families to experience as few problems as possible on the trail, while gaining maximum pleasure from the "trail of togetherness".

This is not a general manual on hiking; it focuses on the *hiking family*. I am not claiming to have written an exhaustive handbook. However, I have — in the light of a little reading that I have undertaken (see the bibliography) and the experience which my wife and I gained over many years of hiking with our four children — attempted to lay down some basic guidelines for hiking families. As is true of hiking in general, it is also true that in family backpacking practice, although often hard, is the best training.

Some of the information in this book was first published (1984) and reprinted (1989) in Afrikaans under the title *Voetslaanavonture vir die gesin*. This is the first English version. Hints for improvement of this English edition will be welcome.

Please note that the prices mentioned for equipment may vary from place to place, depending on from whom you buy them. Also allow for annual inflation.

A word of sincere thanks to my sons, Mias and Barend, who provided some of the beautiful photographs, and George for his drawings.

Your comments will be welcome. My address is:
7 Bezuidenhout Street, Potchefstroom 2520.

So long for the moment, until perhaps one day we can

offer each other a warm hiker's handshake on some trail out in the wilds!

Potchefstroom
October, 1995

Bennie van der Walt

1. BACKPACKING IN GENERAL

I use the word *backpacking* here to indicate that our subject is not merely a matter of going for a stroll. We are gearing you for a hiking trip, an activity which forces hikers to carry with them everything that they are going to need over the walking period.

Backpacking contains at least three elements: a hiker, his/her backpack, and the hiking activity itself. These three elements determine the structure of this book: In the first place I deal with the hikers (in this instance the whole extended family), then the backpack, and in the third place the hiking experience itself.

It is by direct intention that I deal with the hikers first, because I am convinced that the right frame of mind is essential for a successful hiking experience. While this is true of hiking in general, it applies even more to hiking with the whole family.

The pack (what you need for hiking) will be dealt with as a secondary issue. You can enjoy a hiking trip with primitive hiking equipment as long as your mental approach is right. It is useless to have the finest, most modern and most expensive equipment if you are not ready to use it. In this instance also, people are more important than things!

This elementary guide to hiking, however, has not been written for children, but primarily for parents and grandparents, because I think they need it most. If they have the right attitude, there should be no difficulties with the junior members of the family.

Let me explain this by way of example. I have hiked with both adults and children. There is usually a substantial disparity between the two experiences. When hiking with adults, a kilometre must usually be conquered as soon as possible. You generally only stop when it is absolutely essential. The scenery around you often only registers as a green blur, and by the time you reach your destination you have not really seen much.

Hiking with children, on the other hand, means discovering the thousand and one small, interesting details that each kilometre can yield. Although their progress is slow, children notice practically everything: pretty stones, butterflies, insects and worms, a camouflaged chameleon, a toadstool under a rock, the smallest flower, shining dewdrops on leaves, a warbler in the grass, a wagtail on the ground and an eagle floating high above. They hear sounds which do not penetrate adults' consciousness: the rushing of wind and water, the buzzing of bees, the cheerful chirping of birds and the haunting call of the fish eagle.

The lesson which we as grown-ups therefore need to learn — a lesson which our children can teach us — is that we have to readjust our senses to receive nature. If we can become like children again, a rich, rewarding hiking experience awaits us.

Adults find it difficult to relearn the sense of wonder — especially if they have to be taught by children! Usually we see the process of education as one-way traffic: children have to learn from us, and we need not learn anything from them. One of the most important things that you must remember when you hike with the family — and wish to enjoy the experience! — is that children's acute powers of perception make them better observers of nature. They are also good philosophers. They are not content with what they see, they want answers to all the whys and wherefores.

If you want to be infected by your children's or grandchildren's enthusiasm, so that your own experience of nature can be revived and blossom, do not try to turn your hiking trips into mini-marathons!

My wife will smile knowingly when she reads this, as

14

I am still trying hard to practise what I am preaching to you. _

Hiking with the family is a special joy — you need not doubt for one moment that you will reap a rich reward.

But hiking with children and grandparents presents a special challenge to parents. The spiritual demands are far more important than the extra physical demands of having to carry the small children's equipment as well as your own.

Let us examine how parents can acquire spiritual fitness for hiking with a family.

2. THE HIKERS

2.1 PARENTS AND CHILDREN

Whoever still thinks that hiking is no more than physical slogging for kilometre after kilometre is wrong in that assumption; it is captivating and rewarding. However, it is a simple fact that accepting the "slog" to get to the reward will simply not be possible without adequate motivation.

If you want to hike with your family, you have to understand yourself. What is needed first and foremost is self-knowledge, and secondly, some elementary child psychology.

2.1.1 "Know thyself"

Each parent has to ask the following questions of him or herself — and answer them honestly! — before daring to go out on a hiking trail with children. Unless the response is positive in every case, the undertaking should not be considered.

*** Do you have sufficient experience of hiking?**

If the parents have not had previous wilderness experiences on foot, the first attempt should not include children. To the uninitiated hiking may seem simple, but there are many things out on the hiking trail that can only be learnt through hard experience. If you are going hiking with your family, your apprenticeship should already be behind you. If not, it might turn into a nightmarish and even dangerous experience.

It is no pleasure to battle with a portable stove (because you failed to get to know its eccentricities) while four hungry and tired kids heat up the atmosphere around you . . .

Unexpected downpours, hail or even snow can lower your morale and that of your family to zero if you are not adequately prepared. It can also be dangerous. The responsibility of parents who go hiking with their families is doubled or quadrupled, depending on the size of the party.

How do you handle even simple things like inadequate or undrinkable water, insect bites, sunburn, blisters on feet and many more crises with children if you have not had the experience yourself?

Hiking also presupposes that you are reasonably fit. Since this is such an obvious requirement, I am not going to elaborate on this matter. If you are unfit, though, remember that nothing enhances your fitness as quickly as hiking!

*** Do you enjoy hiking?*

Notwithstanding the fair amount of hiking experience of many parents, they may not — in their heart of hearts — really like it. Mother might have hiked indulgently with father before they had children, or father might have gone hiking with a girlfriend who obviously enjoyed it as part of his ploy to win her over.

If the parents are not truly enthusiastic hikers, they should not try to go hiking with their children. Even though hiking is particularly inexpensive, it might in the end be better to opt for a (more expensive) hotel holiday. Children have incredibly fine-tuned antennae, and if they get the least inkling that the parents are not really enjoying it, the hiking trip will turn into torture rather than a joy for all concerned.

The ideal of course, is a mother and father who are

passionate about hiking. I am aware, however, that often one partner is unable to work up boundless enthusiasm at the prospect of slogging across the landscape in heavy boots and encumbered by a bouncing backpack. In such cases it is better for one parent to stay home and leave the other to tackle the wilderness with the children in tow. The other parent could then be indulged by a next holiday in the form of a relaxing time on the beach!

* Are you willing to carry an extra burden?

Family hiking demands of parents physical and spiritual energy and the ability to enjoy things with their children. Perhaps you know the anecdote about the chap who was unmarried, and therefore had no children, never drank, laughed or sang or went on holiday. When he died the insurance company refused to pay out his insurance to his relatives. The reason? He could not be dead, because he had never lived! This reminds me of the words of the famous poet Thoreau: "I went to the woods because I wished to live deliberately, to confront only the essential facts of life . . . and not, when I die, discover that I had not lived."

At the age of fifteen our eldest son was capable of carrying everything he needed himself. At the age of eight our youngest daughter could not yet carry all her own equipment. Should you have one or more smaller children, you must expect to carry a heavier load. This implies that if you are not quite able (because of your degree of unfitness) to cope even with your own load, a hiking trip with the children should not even be attempted.

A hiker is nearly always confronted by the choice between essentials and luxuries. One hiker's essentiality may be the next hiker's luxury, and where children are concerned "luxuries" like toys may become a necessity.

Hiking with children inevitably means extra things and extra weight. Ask yourself honestly whether you would be willing and able to carry not only extra food and clothes, but also in the case of a baby or a toddler, a child on your back.

The additional burden of being a "pack animal" — and a patient one at that! — does not preclude other burdens which you may have to shoulder. The social side is even more important. You have to be a willing and enthusiastic teacher, guide, storyteller, sing-song leader, natural scientist, geologist, nurse, cook and much more for your children. This can be a demanding role indeed, best shared by the parents, but crucially important for the success of the family outing.

* Do you have a positive attitude?

The children should find their parents' enthusiasm for hiking contagious, and this should already be obvious during the preparatory stage. Mom and dad should involve the children in the preparations as far as possible. Tell the children where you are going for the hike, what they might expect to see along the way, why you are packing certain things. Show them the map and explain how the compass and the pedometer work — even though they might not understand everything fully. Teach them how to light a gas stove — even though you might not allow them to cook on it in the wilds. Let your child tie an own pocket knife and whistle to his backpack, or show her the contents of the first-aid box and entrust her with carrying this essential item.

The proof of the pudding lies in maintaining this positive outlook out on the track, in the middle of problems such as heat, cold, rain, dust and mud. You might barely have started walking before Junior loudly demands water. Instead of dismissing him with: "You can't possibly be thirsty yet!" indulge him. He might simply be keen to taste the water from a brook or he is dying to try out his new water bottle. Don't force him to wait — this may irrevocably spoil the beginning of the trip. This is an important point: *Children are usually not tired, but bored. If you keep their thoughts occupied, their legs will keep going!*

* Are you always in a hurry?

I am ashamed to admit that this is one of my own weaknesses, and it is a character trait that is totally at odds with a family hiking trip.

There is often a big difference between the way in which adults and children approach hiking. Grown-ups tend to make a race of it — to their own detriment. Children like to linger and stroll, because there are so many things along the route that they have not seen or heard or smelled or touched before. Their sense of wonder goes into top gear, and quality rather than quantity counts for them. They do not care in the least how **many** kilometres they have done during the past two hours, but rather **how** they have done them, and how many interesting things they have seen.

Family habits can differ a great deal. Let us look at three examples.

The father in family A likes to get going, and he cannot stand the children's dawdling. He is up first in the morning, and takes to the road with the heaviest pack. The other heavy pack he either leaves in the camp or hides somewhere. Mother carries only the lightest pack with absolute essentials that the children might need along the way. Once father has left his own pack at the next point or camp (seven kilometres further), he returns to the camp to fetch the other pack. He may hike the last

20

distance of the final leg along with the family, but mostly he overtakes them for the second time and leaves them behind to go and get the camp in order for wife and children. He therefore covers three times the distance covered by his wife and children — and he enjoys it. This family believes that it is important to be together once camp has been reached, but not necessarily en route.

Family B does not shift camp every day but establishes a base camp for a few days. They then undertake day trips (with light packs) from the camp in order to get to know the area.

When family C starts out, every member adjusts to the speed of the slowest member. The parents have decided that a child under six cannot do more than two kilometres an hour, and for them hiking is not a matter of running a marathon or setting records. Father C believes that hiking is intended to be enjoyed by all and that if he perpetually nags it will spoil the experience for everybody. His philosophy is more or less that of Mahatma Ghandi: "There is more to life than increasing its speed". For that reason, the family often breaks the hike to eat or drink something or to study some interesting natural phenomenon they have come across. At times they may decide to pitch their tent earlier rather than press on to reach their pre-planned stop.

You have to decide for yourself what kind of family you belong to and then choose the best possible recipe for yourself and your family.

* Are you flexible enough?

You planned at the outset that the family would have to cover at least ten kilometres a day so that you can complete the hiking trail in the three days at your disposal. Soon, however, it becomes clear that Susan will definitely not make it. She wants to walk by herself at her own pace, or else she must be carried if you want to cover more ground. You are also gaining the distinct impression that mom's speed is not at all it was supposed to be, but you are not saying anything — yet. If things go on like this, however, you will not complete the trail and you won't even reach the first overnight hut before dark.

My sympathies, my friend! This can be highly frustrating. Just don't show it! This is where you have to be flexible. Don't worry incessantly. Just make the decision, there and then, not to try and finish the whole trail. Who said it was compulsory anyway? And if you are carrying a tent, it is not essential that you sleep in the booked huts.

Don't be too ambitious in your planning, and be willing, even, to reduce your expectations further should this be necessary.

Jack, of course, did not listen to you when you said that he had to wear his shoes at all times, so he stepped into a concealed bottle shard even before you were properly hitting the trail. The whole trip is down the drain. A hiding and a shouting match won't do anything about the deep cut on his foot — and won't save the weekend. You have to accept it. Even if the only solution is to pitch your tents right there on the camping ground at the foothills, this is better than nothing.

Sometimes it might even happen that one of the children forgot to pack hiking shoes at all!

These things force you to make quick and often very innovative plans.

* Are you willing to start from the first grade?

If you are no longer a first-grader, it is hard to do first-grade work and to pretend (like a teacher) that you are actually enjoying it. In family hiking, though, you will have to be willing to start right from scratch and to think small. A superior attitude will not impress the little ones, much less succeed in educating them.

This is true with regard to distance. It also applies to steep and difficult routes.

For a first family hike, the trip should hardly extend over a full weekend. However keen the family might be to sleep out under the stars, this is a no-no if you have not done a day trip together yet. And even if you have, it might be wiser to undertake a first outing to a camp where you will remain comparatively close to civilization when you hike.

Bigger and more ambitious projects should be attempted gradually. The whole experience should be a joy for the children. Never overwhelm them. Even if things seem a little tame for you, consider the children's experience. A child finds huge excitement in drinking out of a water bottle, carrying a rucksack, wearing new hiking shoes, eating out in the wild — even if this lasts only half a day.

I even suggest that you can try out most of your plans at home first. Simply go for a walk in the neighbourhood with your family and see how they fare. (It is necessary, anyway, to "wear in" shoes a little before you go on a big walk.) Pitch your tent in the backyard, and sleep in it after testing it (using the hosepipe) to determine whether it actually is waterproof!

Children are not used to a hiking diet either. It may be a good idea to experiment beforehand. Cook in the back-yard, using the utensils you intend carrying with you, and making your planned recipes. Then select your family members' favourite recipes for the trip. It is important to reserve these meals only for hiking trips — they become part of the whole family hiking ritual!

If you are willing to start in Grade 1, you should develop quickly to expert status. Whatever you do, don't try to kick off in the middle — this might just have the effect of keeping everybody stagnant there.

* Are you innovative enough?

Originality is a real asset to the parents of a hiking family. There are two occasions when this is an essential quality: when you have to acquire hiking gear for the children, and when you have to keep their minds occupied during the trip.

Children's hiking gear is expensive in relation to that of grown-ups, especially when you consider how fast children grow out of things. Their hiking boots don't last a year before they are too small. It is best to start off with a grown-up size sleeping bag, even though it may be necessary at first to sew up the bottom until the children have grown into it.

Apart from the expense, it is difficult to find good hiking gear for children in South Africa. In Europe and the USA one has a wide selection, but in South Africa even the most basic things are unavailable, even in large urban centres. This makes it doubly difficult for hikers living in rural areas to be fitted out. We could not, for example, find an essential item such as a really waterproof raincoat for children locally. In such cases mom and dad have to wrack their brains to find a solution. Mom's sewing machine and dad's toolkit can come in handy in these predicaments.

The second test for innovation is in keeping children occupied. This applies during the entire trip: from the moment when you get into the car, during the hike, in the overnight hut or tents, until you get into the car to go home. Children get bored easily, and bored children are a heavy burden. When you hike, it is impossible to carry a whole load of toys or games, or the TV. You have to depend on your own inventiveness and on what you can find in nature. All the games, riddles, stories and songs found in books can eventually lose their novelty, and then you are out on a limb with only your own imagination!

* Patience, o patience!

Perhaps everything that has been said before can be encapsulated in the one expression: On the trail your patience should outstretch the number of kilometres ahead!

I should, however, end this section on a positive note. Think, for one moment, what a wonderful privilege it is to be able to initiate your children (and perhaps friends of your children who do not share their good fortune) into the wonders and mysteries of nature.

If you are a believer, nature is not simply something which is there — it is the work of God. It is so difficult at times to tell children about an invisible God, but in the mirror of his creation they can concretely experience his greatness, omnipotence and majesty. No human being could make even the simplest little veld flower, not to mention the immeasurable starry skies.

2.1.2 Know your children

Perhaps you have never even considered the need for a fair dash of self-knowledge for happy hiking.

Apart from self-knowledge, it is also necessary to know your children.

I find it a little pretentious to talk about child-psychology, as I cannot speak with any degree of authority on the matter. However, my wife and I have attained a little gut psychology, and you can be the judges as to the usefulness of this "veld psychology"!

You need not only to find correct shoes for your children. You have to, so to speak, enter their shoes and see the world through their eyes. Try to reimagine how a child experiences the world. Try to understand them!

If you succeed in this most difficult of commissions, you are assured of a successful family hike. The lesson seems clear: If there are no problem parents, there won't be problem children along the hiking trail!

Here are some hints, again offered in the shape of examples.

* Not tired — bored!

I have already mentioned this. Children have the most amazing capacity at home or in a playground to cover several kilometres, but on the trail they will soon, sometimes barely after a single kilometre, inform you that they are tired. If father started out too fast, this may well be the case, but mostly the five-year-old is not tired, he has simply been unable to muster the same enthusiasm for the project to which you are so dedicated!

The cure for this tiredness is simply to make the enterprise more interesting for your youngest offspring. Direct his or her attention to everything along the trail that can be seen, heard, smelled, touched or tasted. I won't ever forget how our five-year-old daughter once, on a difficult piece of track, fell behind and completely refused to take another step. Mom diplomatically took her to one side to view the pink heather from closer up, and after a while her tiredness simply vanished. Armed with the additional enticement of a red candy she soon took the lead.

To act as the guide for the children obviously entails preparation in the form of reading about the area and the interesting things to be found there. There are usually all sorts of interesting details on the back of the hiking map, and local libraries are sure to stock books on the flowers, trees, aloes, proteas, ericas, grasses, butterflies, birds, mammals, reptiles, insects, geology and climate of South Africa.

If nature does not offer enough distractions, you can keep the children occupied with songs, word games, riddles and stories.

Remember too that small children are not all that impressed by majestic mountains, mighty rivers and wide panoramas. They are far more fascinated by the small, immediate miracles to be found right at their feet.

* A definite objective strengthens motivation

Children may also lack interest because hiking is, to them, not an end in itself. They want to know where they are going. It is important to name a destination, and to make sure that it is an interesting one! Tell them, for instance, that they are going to sleep in a cave, or that they are going to pitch their new tent for the first time next to a lovely stream (children like water).

Indicate the destination on the map and show them from time to time what progress they are making. If you are carrying a pedometer they can check the distances completed on it. You should also try to have interim objectives along the way, for example: "We are now going to walk up to those huge trees across there, or that funny rock, and when we get to the waterfall, you can each have a piece of chocolate." Or: "We will eat as soon as we have covered another 1 000 metres, so start counting!"

You will be surprised at the amount of energy this can induce in "tired" children.

* Partnership in the team

Children are usually proud of carrying their own backpack (perhaps with their names and some badges on it).

At times, however, they can be decidedly teed off by the burden, and then you have to motivate them by indicating the importance of the specific items they are carrying: the matches, the small gas stove, compass, map, binoculars, field guide, whistle, hunting knife, torch, nylon rope, water bottle, a light lunch and — perhaps most importantly — the cold drink mix and the sweet snacks for the breaks. Do not forget to weigh all the backpacks, so that everybody will know exactly how much he or she is carrying.

There should also be room, in the backpack, for little treasures gathered along the way: pretty stones, grasses, pieces of wood, etc.

Your young companions should feel that they are an important part of the hiking team and have not simply been dragged along because they could not be left at home on their own. This will make them feel infinitely more involved.

What is true out on the trail is equally true when camp is being pitched. Each of the children should have some responsibility. Let baby sister wash the dishes — even though mom may have to wash them all over again (but only once the child has fallen asleep).

A word of praise

Don't forget to enthusiastically give your children credit for their "achievements": "I never thought you were strong enough to carry that heavy backpack all the way up that steep incline — and not a word of complaint! Are you sure you are only nine?" Or: "I haven't tasted such nice coffee in a long time! Clever girl!"

We have also found it to be an effective strategy to let

a tired child take the lead — walking in front is very encouraging!

Apart from this it is important for each member to have an opportunity to point the way — even if it is perfectly obvious. Ask the child to note the indicators (painted feet or other beacons) and to check whether there are spoor or other signs of wild animals.

* Make-belief

Hiking is hard work. It is harder work for the little ones who have to take three steps to every one step of an adult, but you must not allow them to realise this.

Make a game of everything. See who can pick up the most sweet wrappers that other hikers may have dropped along the way. If you want to teach them that nature should be polluted as little as possible when you camp, you can do it in the following way: "Let us pretend that the enemy is on our track. When we break up camp, we have to do it in such a way that nobody will be able to notice that we slept here last night. All signs of our presence have to be wiped out. No scrap of paper, no matches or cigarette butts are to be left lying around. All the stones that we used to secure the tent stakes go back to their original places. Not even the grass should be disturbed!"

* Stick to concrete evidence

I believe that children think in concrete terms, not abstractions. They will be bored by a general lecture about how wonderful insect life is. Rather show them a live beetle, a dung beetle, a grasshopper or a chameleon, and then give them interesting details about the creature in question. Let each of them measure off a square metre of veld, and let them see what they can find in that area:

how many different grasses, veld flowers, stones, ants . . .

When you offer a nature-conservation lesson about the danger of veld fires, tell it in the form of a story about a rabbit family fleeing in front of the flames. Or say something like: "Do you know how many thousands of matches can be made from just one tree — but it takes only one match to burn down the whole tree?"

* Meaningful rules

Children are not averse to rules, but they do need to know *why* they have to obey the rules. If you terrorise them with a lot of do's and don'ts along the trail, and expect them to obey simply because "Daddy says so!", they will not find it fair. Explain to them why soapy water should not be dumped into a river: "In this river (the Treur in the Eastern Transvaal) one finds a rare catfish, which exists only in this part of the world. The least bit of soap in the water will kill it."

In this way we teach our children that we cannot create or recreate nature, but we can and should conserve it.

Or tell the story of the boy who did not listen to his parents when they told him never to run ahead so far that they lose sight of him. He took a wrong turning, got lost and had to spend a long night alone in the veld, without food and water.

Of course, you have to be consistent in setting rules for the veld, and you have to comply with them yourself, otherwise the child will have the fullest right to come to the conclusion that you don't really mean it. Words are effective only insofar as they are backed by deeds.

* With a pinch of salt

Do take their little complaints seriously, because they are serious about them. If Johnny complains about a sore foot, and Helen insists that the shoulder straps are chafing, don't dismiss it with: "That's impossible! We can have a look later." Just paying attention to the little problem usually satisfies the complainant. I remember that my wife brought along that old panacea, Zambuk ointment, and used it to good effect the first time we covered fifteen kilometres a day in the Drakensberg. A quick rub with the fragrant menthol ointment cured all ailments in sight!

It suggests, doesn't it, that a little calculated whitewash will go a long way in effecting a cure . . .

* Complete acceptance

I have told you how important it is that each child should be made to feel a welcome, important member of the hiking team. It is equally important that each child should be fully accepted as a human being, each with an own personality, limitations and needs.

Before the trip begins, it is important to realise — and accept — that all members of the family are not equally strong, fit and brave. Hiking is a sure-fire way of revealing strengths and weaknesses in equal measure.

If Peter is by nature a little aggressive, he could easily explode when things get a little difficult on the trail. If George does not like curry or raisins, mom should not expect him suddenly to like them if dished up on the trip. When Mom buys sweets for the trip, she should remember that not everybody is nuts about chocolate.

This reciprocal acceptance is not only applicable to parents and children. Children should also develop mutual tolerance towards each other. If the one is a fanatic bird lover, the other who likes flowers should not say: "You and your old birds! What do you see in them anyway?" Older brothers have to understand and accept that younger brothers cannot yet do what they can do themselves.

The hiking trail is narrow enough to necessitate a sense of coherence. If everybody has to crawl into a small tent at night, it is essential not to rub one another up the wrong way!

The veld is also wide enough, however, to offer one another living space, so that everybody can simply be himself or herself.

2.1.3 Know the limits

I would like to conclude this section with a few questions about limits. In other words, that which is possible and that which is not possible. You have to keep in mind that the responses to these questions will depend greatly on the individual circumstances — conclusive answers which are applicable to all families, are just not possible.

* How soon can I begin hiking with my children?

The answer is that you can already start taking a small baby along on a hike. This will depend entirely on the health of the baby, the condition of the mother, the environment, the climate and the equipment available.

Babies are usually easy hiking companions. They do have to be carried all the time, of course.

Toddlers from one to three years old can be difficult. Usually they don't want to be carried all the way, but then they can't walk all that far either and tend to put everything they can lay their hands on into their mouths!

Three- to four-year-olds can be a joy as hiking companions.

We only began hiking when our youngest was five years old, so we don't really have experience of the very young ones. We did encounter such families along the trail, however — and you can learn a great deal from books!

* What distance can a family cover in a day?

Another difficult question. Our daughter of five could cover fifteen kilometres a day over easy terrain, but could not really sustain this for longer than two days. It is important that when the family goes hiking, their plans should provide for "free" days to allow the children — and the parents! — a breather.

At present our family's average speed (excluding lunch break) is about three kilometres per hour, that is plus minus 20 minutes per kilometre.

For a family with small children I would not really consider doing more than two kilometres per hour.

* How much can the children carry?

I have already stressed that *what* a child carries is far more important to him than *how much* he carries. Parents would like to know, however, how soon and how much of his or her own pack a child can carry.

Our own experience is that **age** is not as important as **being used to** the backpack. I still distinctly remember our first hiking trip, which disintegrated into one great clamour and complaint! However, as everyone became used to the weight on shoulders and back, the complaining subsided.

I would say that one cannot really expect a pre-school child to carry a weight of any significance. At the age of about fifteen or sixteen, however, children can be considered mature backpackers. Our son was able at the age of fourteen, to cope with nearly the same weight as his father could.

The exact weight also depends on the child's physical condition and body weight. For smaller children (from the age of six to early teens) it should not be more than one-fifth of their body weight.

From the age of fifteen, however, they can easily, as do grown-ups, carry one-third of their own body weight.

* How much does it cost to go hiking with the family?

Most of us have budgetary constraints, and therefore this is an entirely legitimate question. Because detailed information will be given in the next chapter, I only provide a rough indication here.

Accommodation costs on a hiking trail are minimal. If you reserve time on one of the national hiking trails at the National Hiking Way Board, Care of: Department of Water Affairs and Forestry, Private Bag X313, Pretoria 0001 (tel. 012-2993382), it can cost as little as R15,00 per night per adult, and R7,50 per child or pensioner. If you go hiking with your own tent in one of the wilderness areas, the permit will only cost about R5,00 per person per day.

It is usually the hiking equipment which cleans out your wallet. If parents already have the basic equipment (tent, cooking and eating utensils), only the children need to be equipped. The expensive items are the backpack, sleeping bag, shoes and a watertight raincoat. But these items are also crucial, and it is foolish to be penny-wise and pound-foolish on them. As I have already indicated, children's hiking equipment is difficult to obtain in this country, and particularly expensive, especially when one considers how soon the children will outgrow these.

When you estimate your expenses, it may be a good idea to distinguish between once-off and annual expenses — then the figure is not so prohibitive!

Prices will, of course, depend on size and quality, and the place and outlet where you buy. Prices given here merely serve as a rough indication.

Among the once-off expenses you should look at are sleeping bags and backpacks.

Good, down-filled sleeping bags are not cheap. Expect prices ranging from R300 - R1 000, depending on your taste and requirements. As already indicated, you should buy an adult size so that the child grows into it instead of out of it.

For the same price (about R300 - R600) you can also buy a backpack. Children can, from the age of ten onwards, carry the small adult backpack and use this for at least five years and longer. If it is available, you can buy your five-year-old a special children's day-pack (about R100) which can also be used for about five years.

A good, waterproof raincoat or waterproof windbreaker can also be bought to last for more than one year. The price of such an item is about R130 - R150.

Our experience has been that shoes have to be replaced annually, or even more often. Real hiking boots can be expensive (from R250 - R1 000) and children's sizes are not readily available in South Africa. We therefore bought our children ordinary running shoes (at about R100 per pair) which gave excellent service and could be replaced fairly cheaply as they wore out or were outgrown.

The total outlay per child (depending on the size and quality of what you buy) therefore comes to around R800 - R1000.

Regarding meals, we have found that providing R12 - R15 per person per day should be ample.

The only outstanding item is the petrol to get you to the hiking trail, but this is an expense that you cannot avoid when going on any holiday.

We have found that although the initial costs may be quite high they tend to even out, and calculated over a few years, backpacking is one of the cheapest holidays around.

A final hint regarding the purchase of backpacks, sleeping bags and tents. These are expensive items, especially when you have to equip a family of six. Do not make the mistake we had made in the beginning to buy whatever was cheapest. Our inferior purchases had to be replaced pretty soon, while products of good quality could have given us a lifetime of sterling service.

2.2 SENIOR CITIZENS

A family includes, as the people of Africa believe, at least three generations: apart from the children with their parents, also the grandparents.

Three aspects need our attention: (1) *Why* seniors should consider hiking as an option. (2) *How* they can make sure that they enjoy hiking. (3) Some suggestions for *when* they do not hike with their age group, but as part of the family.

2.2.1 Hiking: an ideal form of recreation for seniors

Most forms of sport can only be practised until you reach a certain age. Hiking is an exception to this rule. One can engage in this sport from before the age of one year (in a baby carrier), up to the age of seventy-five or even longer.

Because people differ, it is also difficult to define "old age". Some people may look old from the "outside", but may not be so "inside". Some may be enjoying good health, while others are not as fortunate. The normal age of "retirement" (at about 60 or 65) is taken as the point of entry into "senior citizenship" — provided one keeps in mind that "retirement" is a phenomenon of the recent past. Not so long ago the retirement habit was unknown. Older people simply continued with their regular occupation up to the point when *they themselves* wanted to take life more slowly!

In various communities and cultures we encounter a variety of myths about old age. We want to briefly examine a few of these, since "elderly" people may tend to accept these stereotypes.

People past the age of sixty are regarded as:

* *Sickly:* affected by arthritis, nearly deaf or blind — or both — and ailing.
* *Inactive:* they only want to sit in an armchair, chatting about the "good old days" or gossipping about their neighbours.
* *Senile:* their brains and memories do not function so well any more.
* *Unproductive:* worn out, useless, worthless, not able to contribute anything more to society.
* *Untidy:* sloppy, careless about their appearance.
* *Isolated:* they have lost contact with their friends, families and society at large, experiencing terrible loneliness.
* *Bored:* they don't know how to utilize their leisure, experiencing life as totally meaningless.
* *Unhappy:* depressed, miserable, spiritless, cheerless, complaining, embittered, stingy, self-centred, etc.

Of course some "elderly" people may fit the above discription(s). I refuse, however, to believe that old age *should be* like this. I know older people who are a living challenge to these stereotypes!

Instead of being pessimistic or — the opposite — too optimistic about this part of our life span, let us be realistic.

* Your body

It is a simple fact that, when you grow older, all kinds of ailments will appear: shortness of breath, difficulties to hear and see, a slower heartbeat, as well as restricted movement of the legs and arms. In most cases this does not exclude physical activity. The only difference is a decrease of physical fitness and a need to take life at a slower pace.

I am not aware of any kind of sport which suits this stage of life better than hiking! If you have any doubts about it, I can mention quite a few examples to prove my point. In the *Introduction* to this book I mentioned the name of Grandma Gatewood, who at the age of 77 completed a solo hiking trip on the 3 200 kilometre Appalachian Trail in the USA.

A South African, Stanley Shuttleworth, describes in his booklet *Age need not weary you* how he, already in his seventies, together with a group of elderly friends undertook various hiking trips in our country.

General Jan Smuts climbed Table Mountain at the age of 80. Reg Pearse, well-known writer of books on the Natal Drakensberg, tackled Sterkhorn (2 973 metres) when he was 90 years old, accompanied by his son and grandson.

* Your activities

People who know, emphasise the importance for retired people not to sit down, waiting upon death, but to stay active. Inactivity leads to decline! Hiking, again, is the ideal: not too little, but also not too strenuous an exercise. Hiking is not merely a physical activity, it offers a much richer experience.

* *Your intellectual ability*

Sophocles wrote his most famous drama (*Oedipus*) at the age of 80 and Bernard Shaw his last when he was 90! Arthur Rubenstein still enjoyed packed audiences at his piano concerts at the age of 90. Ann Mary Robertson, without any training in the fine arts, started painting at 76, continuing till the age of 100! I have not even mentioned the names of a whole list of people — including our State President, Nelson Mandela — who only reached the apex of their political careers in their seventies.

* *Your productivity*

Many retired people start a second career. Others prefer to practise their favourite hobbies which they previously neglected because of the demands of a full-time job. For them, life starts after sixty — sometimes by discovering the joys of hiking.

* *Your involvement*

Gerontologists (experts on ageing) emphasise the fact that elderly people must stay in contact with their environment and with other people, because of the danger that their world may shrink to include only themselves and their afflictions. Retirees should not only be involved with their own peer group, but especially also with younger people. The most recent tendency in caring for older people is to keep them inside a family unit for as long as possible instead of moving them into old-age homes. Economic realities and government policy currently favour this.

Hiking provides seniors with an ideal opportunity to have contact with a wide variety of people: those who accompany you on your hike — your children and grandchildren, or a group of other people of your age; and those whom you encounter along the hiking route or at overnight stops.

The social aspects of hiking which are so important for young people, are perhaps even more important for seniors.

* Using leisure time usefully

Freed from all kinds of responsibilities towards dependents and from the restrictions previously imposed by your vocation, you now probably enjoy much more leisure. If you do not know how to use this extra time, free time could easily become boredom.

May I again recommend hiking as the best medicine? It is not a primitive, uncivilized activity as many non-hikers may think. Hikers have, in the course of time, developed a variety of interests: in the rich fauna of our country (insects, birds an animals); in the even richer flora (trees, shrubs, flowers and grasses); the interesting history of different parts of the country; the language, customs and cultures of people in the different regions; and much more.

Hiking in nature provides thousands of opportunities for the photographer, painter, writer and poet . . . You will always be surprised by something new to see, hear, experience or learn.

* The multi-dimensional recreation

Hiking has therapeutic value because it is not a one-dimensional activity. Consider, among other things, the following aspects:

Hiking is healthy: The moderate exercise it provides is exactly what the heart, lungs and other muscles of an

older person needs. Experts agree that walking, including extended walking in the form of hiking, is the best possible exercise to prevent many ailments (like osteoporosis) which are regarded as "typical" of elderly people.

 # Hiking allows you to breathe freely again: It enables you to leave your room or flat to experience the open spaces and see wide horizons.

 # Hiking sensitizes all your senses: You will discover again that you have eyes, a nose, taste and other senses. It can also unburden you of the excess baggage of emotional tension, stress, depression and other complaints.

 # Hiking makes you think clearly: My own experience has been that a hiking trip is good not only for my legs but also for my brain. With enough exercise, fresh air, enough sleep and good food it is impossible not to get a new perspective on matters.

 # Hiking improves your interpersonal relationships: Hikers are seldom stricken by dumbness: they usually have too much to talk about — prior, during and after a hiking trip. Along the way, new and solid friendships are established.

 # Hiking evokes the artist in you: You can take photographs, collect leaves, grasses and flowers; you can paint, draw, write down the history of a place or region or simply keep a diary of the entire hiking trip.

 # Hiking is economical: The minimal expense involved is nothing against the fortune you will have to spend at a hotel. You do not have to worry about a deficit in your monthly pension.

Hiking opens up windows on eternity: When you become older, you start thinking about death more often. Nobody with honest, open eyes will walk in nature without being reminded of the Creator of it all. What a wonderful opportunity to be able, in the paradise of nature, to prepare yourself for Paradise on the new earth!

Summarized: hiking brings you to life, real life: Hiking can definitely improve the quality of life also of our senior citizens. The only condition is a correct attitude. A positive attitude towards life is the great secret behind happiness and contentment.

2.2.2 How to make sure that you enjoy your hiking experience

Most of the advice given earlier in this book also applies to older hikers. What is given here may be considered as obvious, common sense. But it can do no harm to remind you pertinently.

* *Hiking experience*

If you were a regular hiker you would know how to adapt to your physical frailties without much difficulty. If you are a novice, however, you should be willing to learn. Be careful not to attempt a route that may be beyond your physical capabilities.

* *Hiking comrades*

Your fellow-hikers will, to a great extent, determine the quality of your hiking experience.

They may be (1) people of your age group, (2) your own family or (3) another group or family.

In the first instance you will be able to take it slowly. The second type of hike could be much faster and also more eventful because of the presence of younger people. In the third case you may be in for even more surprises.

An older person should not easily join just any group. Personally, I shall either hike with my own age group consisting of people I already know, or with my own children and grandchildren.

The simple message is: Make sure that you will fit into the group, and prepare yourself. Decide beforehand that you will be patient and not get angry with your energetic — and often naughty — grandchildren.

* Physical fitness

Like any other hiker you should not try a hiking trip without a fair amount of fitness. It is a simple fact that, even if you are reasonably fit for your age, you are no longer capable to do what you could achieve at the age of 25. To walk too long distances or uphill too fast is not advisable.

* Limitations

Because of these inevitable limitations of older age it is good advice to start slowly, especially if you are undertaking serious hiking for the first time. First try a brief walk of a few hours. If this goes well, then try a whole day with some weight (a day-pack) on your shoulders. You may decide that this is enough for you, or you may become confident to attempt a longer hike of three days carrying a backpack on your shoulders.

Senior hikers should remember that hiking trails in South Africa are designed for young and middle-aged people and not for older people.

I would suggest that our National Hiking Way Board provide a list of hiking routes (or sections of these routes) suitable for hikers of sixty years old and older.

* Food, medicine and clothes

Young people can eat almost anything. Older people have to be more careful. Because your meals on a hiking trip will be different from regular meals at home, it is important to choose your provisions carefully, to try them out at home and to plan your hiking meals in advance. Please remember *always* to take emergency rations along.

You may have to take medicine (like blood pressure pills) on a daily basis. Please make sure that you do not leave these at home, and take along enough. At this stage of your life you are already aware of the ailments which may suddenly occur and spoil your trip — be prepared. The regular first-aid kit should be taken along.

Because of different circumstances under hiking conditions, special precautions will have to be taken with spectacles, dentures, hearing aids, and so on. Ensure that these can be carried and stored safely.

Senior hikers may also need special clothing. Because of a sensitive skin a special hat with a broad rim and a flap at the back to keep out the ultraviolet rays of the sun may be neccessary — anti-sunburn creams are usually not enough. Don't be disdainful of a walking stick. I have always found my "kierie" a valuable companion and I imagine that, as I become older, I will appreciate it even more.

When I was younger I could easily fall asleep with only a thin groundsheet under me. Lately I prefer a more comfortable foam mattress!

Security

I have met senior hikers hiking without any companions. I do not think it is wise to walk alone — not even for young hikers. Apart form the fact it is much more sociable to hike in a group, one should also be aware of the safety factor. I do not only have in mind possible "natural" accidents. We all know that increasingly nowadays older people are becoming the targets of muggers and even murderers.

On the other hand, there is no reason to be unduly afraid. Attacks usually happen in the so-called "civilized" areas of our country (towns, cities and homesteads on farms). I have thus far not heard of a single elderly person being attacked on a hiking route!

Focus

Hiking for the younger generation mostly tends to become a physical challenge: the fifteen kilometres have to be completed in the shortest possible time! Of course also for seniors hiking remains a challenge — otherwise part of the adventure is lost. You will not want to be spared the sore back and painful feet at the end of the day.

With "focus" I am simply reminding our senior hikers that they should approach their hiking experience from an adult perspective. A senior hiker will rest regularly along the way to prevent over-exhaustion. Remember that hiking is not a physical activity only. Deliberately explore the many other interests on a hiking trip.

2.2.3. Some suggestions when you are hiking with a family

This book is about backpacking adventures for the family and it includes not only children and parents, but also grandparents.

I now want to have the attention of the parents. They have a dual responsibility: on the one hand towards their children and on the other hand towards their parents. In the first part of this book the responsibility of taking children along was discussed at length. I give only a few suggestions about taking seniors along — because in many cases this second responsibility will not differ totally from the first!

* Be prepared to adjust your speed

If you want to go too fast, your parents will not enjoy the hike, and consequently, neither will you.

* Be willing to help them to carry their equipment

Sometimes a strong, teenage grandson will be willing to help grandfather carry his backpack up a steep incline. It may even be advisable to distribute grandmother's gear right from the start among the backpacks of the younger generation.

* Be considerate

Acknowledge — as in the case of your children — the special needs and interests of the older people.

* Be patient with their special needs

Older people sometimes need more warmth. Therefore take along an extra space blanket — even if they do not consider it necessary. Older people are likely to be frail and their bone structure brittle — do not attempt difficult hikes. Often they cannot see so well any more — take along a magnifying glass to help them watch the small flowers and insects.

* *Be ready to accommodate their sometimes peculiar habits*

Because of less control of the bladder, they may have to go to the "toilet" more often. They are used to their beds at home and cannot fall asleep on the ground as easily as the kids — provide them with an inflatable mattress. Please, do not get upset — not even when they snore at night!

* *Be willing to learn from them*

Do not think — and even give the impression! — that you do not have to listen to what they have to say. They do not want to be a lonely appendix to a hiking trip arranged primarily for yourself and your children. They want to be part of the adventure.

* *Be prepared*

Because you know beforehand that you have to accommodate — in an enjoyable and peaceful way — ages from seven to seventy, it is a good idea not to wait until problems crop up on the trip. Have a planning meeting of the whole extended family prior to the trip to discuss possible tensions in an open and frank way. If everyone in the party knows in advance what he/she is up to and exactly what his/her responsibilities are, you will be in a much better position to accommodate the frustrations of the younger, faster ones as well as the capacities of the older, slower ones!

2.2.4. Conclusion

My sincere wish is that this brief chat has succeeded in removing some misconceptions and even fears about growing older and hiking as a senior citizen. I do hope that the result will be that I will soon meet more grey-heads, like myself, on our beautiful hiking ways.

Hiking with a group of energetic, vivacious teenage boys offers a unique experience. Hiking with a family is different. And different again will be a hiking group consisting only of people of above 60 years of age. The fact, however, that it is different, does not imply that it will be less enjoyable. If it is well planned, it could be interesting and adventurous. Hiking offers its own pleasures for every generation!

I do not underestimate for one moment the challenge of hiking with the whole extended family. At the same time it can be one of the richest and most rewarding experiences in life. In this time of disintegration of families, we need family activities like this.

Do not wait any longer. Have a chat with your husband/wife, your children or your senior neighbours. Discuss with friends or acquaintances in your old-age home the possibility of a hiking club for seniors. And please inform me about the results — I want to prepare myself for hiking after sixty! My wife and I hope to become grandparents in the near future. And one of our desires is one day to be able to enjoy the privilege of a hiking trip with our grandchildren!

Perhaps your reaction, having read up to here, is: "Why deal so extensively with the hikers? I would like to know more about the equipment I need!" Let me repeat what I said right at the beginning: The hikers, the people, are the most important component. They need to have the right attitude and approach. The equipment is an accessory - albeit an essential one — to make the whole trip more comfortable.

The time has now come to talk about the pack you are going to carry on your back, and then the actual hiking activity will be discussed.

3. THE BACKPACK

This chapter does not deal only with the rucksack and its contents. You must think of all the other equipment, such as a baby carrier, a tent, and all the paraphernalia that go into the pack.

The subsections in this chapter are:
* the hiking outfits for the family, including the grand-parents
* the pack (rucksack) in which everything (including your baby) is transported
* everything that goes into the rucksack and how this has to be used.

Firstly, then, a word about what you have to wear.

3.1 THE HIKING OUTFIT

Clothes are not intended for covering and decoration only, they also protect you against the elements — the latter characteristic being of particular importance during a hike. Your clothes have to protect you against cold, heat, rain, wind, plants and insects.

* In the cold

When dressing children — and adults — it is important to use the layering system: a layer of air is trapped between the body and the first layer of clothing, and this is repeated for each subsequent layer of clothing as air is trapped between each two layers. Somebody wearing an undershirt, T-shirt, track suit and windbreaker is far more effectively dressed against the cold than somebody wearing simply a heavy coat or a quilted windbreaker. Temperature can be regulated more easily by simply removing one or more layers of clothing.

This is especially important in the case of children who have to be carried. They are not walking and generating heat, so they have to be dressed warmly.

You lose a great deal of body heat through your scalp. It is, therefore, essential that children should wear caps or balaclavas in cold weather — especially at night, when the temperature drops rapidly. A general proverb among hikers is: "If your feet are cold, cover your head!"

The best textile to wear is wool or cotton. Wool is mostly expensive, however, and personal taste also plays an important role. Any kind of material which is soft and pliant as well as an effective absorbent will be suitable.

I chose to begin my discussion with protection against the cold, because exposure to cold, leading to hypothermia, is one of the greatest dangers faced by hikers. (This happens when your body loses more heat than it generates and your internal body temperature drops.) Keep in mind that children lose body heat much more rapidly than adults.

Heat

A hiker should not only be ready for cold, he should also be prepared for other climatic conditions. Without adequate head and body covering the heat of the sun can be dangerous. A good hat is important — with a broad rim and a flap at the back to cover the neck. People with a sensitive skin can even take along a lightweight, foldaway umbrella.

Wearing light colours is sensible as they deflect sunlight. I have never, however, encountered a hiker in pure white (like a tennis player or a pharmacist) because one is faced with a delicate choice: comfort or cleanliness? Light colours are cooler but they show the dirt that much sooner. Darker colours may not be as cool, but they look cleaner for longer. One has to find an acceptable compromise here, and we have found khaki to be most suitable.

You always have to carry a sunscreen cream, and it may be advisable for some children to wear dark glasses in strong sunlight. "Sun tablets" have to be taken according to prescription.

* Rain

Getting wet is uncomfortable and your clothes will lose their insulation ability. You can soon become very chilly. Rainclothes should therefore never — even outside the rainy season — be left behind.

Don't be satisfied with ordinary raincoats (e.g. school raincoats). Most everyday raincoats are not really waterproof as the seams are sewn together. They cannot withstand a real shower. The seams must be fused or covered by watertight strips of rubber or something similar.

We had great difficulty in obtaining good raincoats for the children, and finally gave up. For the youngest two we bought fishermen's jackets at the local co-operative store (the same yellow or orange jackets worn by roadworkers). Although they were small sizes they were still large enough for the children not to need separate pants!

The older members of the family did not have a problem. We could obtain proper rain jackets and pants made of a soft and light material and they are comfortable indeed.

If you can find waterproofed light nylon material (urethane or something similar), it may be better to consider making the children's rainwear yourself.

The easiest pattern is a poncho. It is simply a triangular piece of material with a hole for the neck and a hood to cover the head. Experiment with a piece of brown paper or newspaper or cheap plastic from a garbage bag until you have the right size for the child's head and then cut out the pattern. The hood can be tightened around the head with a string threaded through the front hem which can be tied beneath the chin in rainy weather. The front parts of the poncho should overlap far enough to prevent rain from coming in — strips of velcro could be used for this purpose. If the back of the poncho is cut big enough, the backpack can also be protected against the rain.

The hiker is faced with another dilemma here. A rain jacket and trousers are more watertight, but may cause condensation problems. Do not be surprised if you become drenched with sweat inside a watertight suit. Because a poncho hangs loosely around the body, the condensation problem may be less acute but you can easily get drenched from below. You will have to weigh up the possibilities and decide whether you want to get wet from outside or from inside! Fortunately children do not perspire as much as grown-ups, so it remains important for you to see to it that their rain gear is really watertight.

One not only gets wet from above, of course. Raindrops or dewdrops on the grass can soak through your pants and run down into your boots so that boots and socks are soon drenched. Rain pants and watertight boots can help somewhat — but you can never keep totally dry!

See next page for poncho pattern.

* Wind

When rain is accompanied by wind the temperature can drop rapidly. Rain gear can provide adequate protection against wind. If you have enough money and space in the rucksack — and the courage to carry all of this! — you

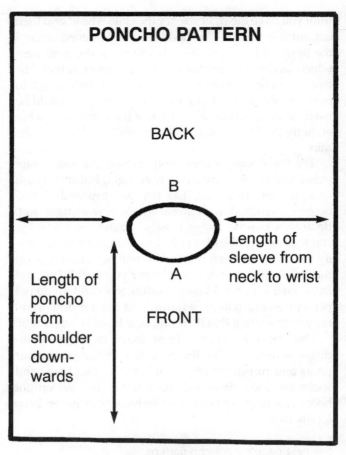

PONCHO PATTERN

BACK

B

A

Length of sleeve from neck to wrist

Length of poncho from shoulder downwards

FRONT

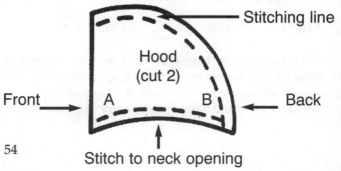

Stitching line

Hood (cut 2)

Front → A B ← Back

Stitch to neck opening

54

may consider buying yourself an extra watertight wind-breaker. Many of them are beautifully quilted.

* From head to toe

Head coverings are important against the heat and cold.

In the same way, good shoes are important. Your are, after all, on your feet all the time. Real hiking boots for children — made of real leather, with the necessary support for the ankles, thick sturdy soles, and hooks rather than holes for shoelaces so that the feet won't get wet easily — are hard to find in South Africa if you live in a rural town. This is especially true of younger children. Older children may be able to find a fit among the women's sizes. Buying good shoes for the children can be expensive, because they grow out of them so soon.

I therefore repeat my recommendation to buy good, comfortable running shoes with good rubber soles. They can use these also for netball, athletics or tennis. There is a wide variety of these on the market.

It is important to buy thick, strong socks, and it is essential to try on the socks with the shoes. I also recommend that you take along at least one pair of clean socks for each day of the trip.

Women and children may want to consider wearing cotton gloves to protect them against prickly and spiny grasses and shrubs, and against sunburn. When it turns cold, though, woollen gloves are required.

* Full protection

On a hiking trip your clothes protect you against the elements and against prickly grasses, spiny shrubs and bushes, insects stings and even snakebite. For that reason, and also to help prevent sunburn, it is preferable both in winter and in summer that you wear long trousers and even long-sleeved shirts. In cold weather I like wearing a T-shirt under a shirt and a short-sleeved khaki bushjacket over it. You can unbotton the bushjacket when it starts getting warm, and the jacket has lots of pockets — something you really need on a trip. My khaki trousers also have, apart from the normal side and back pockets, a long pocket down each side which can be used for small items.

* Special needs of babies

I do not recommend hiking with babies and small toddlers during winter. Even during spring and summer one has to be prepared for cold. Because they are carried and do not generate body heat, little ones need more layers of clothing. According to the experts, a hand-knitted one-piece suit which covers the child from neck to toe is most suitable. One-piece stretch suits known as baby-gro's (without a hood) are also acceptable. A cotton vest under it gives an additional isolation layer in the cold, and absorbs perspiration when it is hot.

As I do not really have experience of hiking with babies, I will leave other coverings to your resourcefulness!

You will have to decide on the kind of nappies you are going to take along: ordinary nappies or disposable ones. The ordinary ones are perhaps more absorbent and less irritating, but what do you do with all the wet and soiled nappies? Disposable nappies, on the other hand, are not really disposable, as they are not really biodegradable, and they can therefore become a pollutant. You will have to burn them — but wet nappies do not really burn. It probably is best to bury them if you cannot put them in a bin at an overnight spot.

Feeding a baby on the trail can also be a headache, as you have to take along all the bottles and feeds. If you are taking only powdered milk and empty bottles, it is a lighter load, but it can take quite some time to boil the water for the feeds. If you fill the bottles before starting out, it will be quicker and easier along the route, but the extra weight will be considerable. This is another interesting challenge for the committed hiker — and one more instance where the breast-feeding mother has reason to smile!

I have found parents happily hiking with babies, so if you follow your protective instincts all will probably be well!

* The minimum clothes with which you can get along

I have come across hikers who carry along pyjamas and slippers, but I must confess I find this a bit much. One has to pay dearly in terms of space and weight for this small comfort. The other extreme is a friend of mine who swears that his T-shirt has four clean sides and that it can therefore be worn four days in a row. The first day it is worn normally. The second day it is worn back to front. Then the shirt is turned inside out, and worn front to back and finally back to front . . .

One need not get into a sleeping bag with sweaty clothes. You can sleep in the set of clean clothes intended for the next day's hike, and children get used to this pattern surprisingly quickly. All that is important is being able to sleep in clean and warm things. A track suit (carried along for cold days) makes excellent pyjamas.

I do not regard clean outer things (shirt, trousers) essential for every day. Clean underwear, on the other hand, is vital, and it takes up little room and weighs little.

When the whole family goes along, you have to carry a lot of extras anyway. Taking too many luxuries is not a good idea as these will encumber you and will not contribute in any real sense to the enjoyment of the trip.

3.2 PACKS IN WHICH TO CARRY EVERYTHING

Let us first look at the backpacks for parents, then for children and finaly packs in which children can be carried.

Backpacks for grown-ups

Parents and grandparents who have never hiked need not reel back in dismay at the thought of carrying a rucksack. True, the old types of backpacks were a real hassle on long trips and they were probably only designed for truly strong people. They were made of heavy canvas, with all the weight hanging from the shoulders, and the hiker had to lean forward at an awkward angle so as not to be pulled backward.

However, nowadays chafed shoulders and a sore back are no longer inevitable when you carry a pack. Modern rucksacks are lighter and are mounted on an aluminium frame which holds it away from the body. It has nylon webbing to protect the part of the back which does come into contact with the rucksack. There are different sections which close with zips and this facilitates better packing. The most important improvement, however, is the way in which the weight is proportionally distributed. The hip belt allows about 75% of the weight to rest on the hips rather than hanging from the shoulders. Practically the only function of the shoulder straps is to keep the rucksack in position. A further improvement is the quilted shoulder and hip straps, which protect you against chafing.

I mention these improvements to provide specific guidelines, so that when you buy a rucksack you will know for what features you must look. Please check that the pack is made of a good quality material; that it has sturdy plastic zippers and not metal ones; nylon webbing for the back which can be tightened if it should become less supportive; that the flap closes not with laces but with nylon tape and buckles which are easy to open and close; that the buckles of the hip belt enable you to loosen and tighten the belt quickly and easily; and that the shoulder straps are easy to adjust without having to take off the backpack.

A backpack with an adjustable frame is the best buy.

In any event, you should never buy a backpack before trying it on, because you have to carry it with you as a tortoise does its shell!

Quite a large variety of backpacks can be found in the shops. You can also buy the frameless type (which has reinforcement inside the bag). The advantages are that it is even lighter than the type with the frame and it may be more stable because it can be worn against the body and move with the body. It is also easier to pack into a crowded car or tent. One possible disadvantage is that it clings more closely to the body, so less air can circulate and you can become more sweaty.

The important thing is to buy the best quality that you can possibly afford. If you are hiking with your whole family, buy a big one (for example, 80 litre capacity), because you have to lug along a lot of the children's things quite apart from your own gear.

Remember that the packs come in small, medium and large sizes, and that the capacity is indicated in litres. Bright colours are attractive and they may even be useful if you lose your way and need to be spotted, but they tend to show dirt more easily. A difficult choice!

The price? For R300 - R600 you can probably buy a large rucksack of fairly good quality.

Children's rucksacks

The selection is limited when you want to buy children's rucksacks in South Africa — particularly for the five- to ten-year-olds.

Initially our daughter of five simply used her school bag. It was rather more for show and to make her feel useful, because one could not pack a great deal in it!

For the older boys we bought the smaller frame sacks (a cheap type) at a sale. They did not have hip belts, and the smallest belts we could find in the shop were still far too large. The rucksacks hung too low on their hips because the shoulder straps were not intended for children. We solved this problem by buying strips of foam from an upholsterer and fixing them with rubber bands to the belt and the shoulder straps.

Frameless rucksacks for children of about 10 - 16 years have since become available. Their capacity varies between 20 and 50 litres. I would recommend the type with strips down the sides so that extra items can be added once the child is able to carry more. You should be able to buy a good (frameless) rucksack for a child for about R100-R300.

Equipment in which to carry your child(ren)

Two types of equipment should be distinguished here.

For a small baby who cannot yet hold up its head on its own, there is a series of slings. You can carry a baby from the age of about a week up to two and a half years in these, either kangaroo-style in front, or African style on the back. These have a quilted headrest which can be taken off for tiny babies, or folded in. Such a baby carrier weighs little (about 250 grams), and it is completely washable.

Another type is for babies and young toddlers who

can sit independently. For them you need a baby carrier with an aluminium frame carried on your back. During my quest I came across only one such a carrier. It weighs about a kilogram and the price at present is R105.

In this specific model the child can only face forward. Some people maintain that this is ideal, since the child likes being close to the parent, and to see who is carrying him. Other experienced people hold the view that it may be better for the child to be able to look backwards. This gives him more leg room, and there is less danger of being struck in the face by a branch. The disadvantage, however, is that the child may refuse to ride like that if there is no family member behind to keep him company. Other experts feel that the backward pull of carrying a child who is looking backwards places more pressure on the parent's shoulders.

Always keep in mind that it is impossible to carry both a backpack and a baby carrier on your back!

Most South African hiking equipment needs further refinement. One carrier which I inspected, for instance, does not have quilted shoulder straps and hip belts. It also does not have straps to secure the child in the carrier, and if you bend forward suddenly, the child can fall out. It can also be made into a far more useful item by adding compartments for carrying things like nappies and clothes. The manufacturer can even add additional fastenings, as on an ordinary rucksack, for sleeping gear. With a little ingenuity parents can make quite a few improvements themselves.

3.3 WHAT HAS TO GO INTO AND ONTO THE BACKPACK?

This makes up quite a long list: your house (tent), your kitchen (cooking and eating utensils), your larder (food), your bathroom (toiletries), your pharmacy (first-aid kit), your wardrobe (clothes), your bed (sleeping bag and mattress) and many more essentials. How on earth do you manage all this — even if the rucksack has a 100-litre capacity?

A few general hints

Firstly, a few general hints about how the rucksack should be packed.

* See that you know exactly where you pack every item

This is especially essential when packing not only for yourself but for children as well. If you are unable to retrieve something because you have forgotten where you packed it, you can create chaos on the trail. You may find yourself faced with the task of unpacking **everything** from your rucksack (and those of the others!) to find the item for which you are looking. It is useful to make a list on a strong piece of paper of what goes into each bag. This entails a little extra effort, but is well worth the trouble.

* Pack things which you need often, where you can find them easily

Your raincoat, camera, films, map, first-aid box and many other things should not go in the bottom of the backpack. Don't pack lunch on top of breakfast either! It may happen that you need a flashlight urgently at night, and if you can't remember where it was packed you can have a real hassle.

*Pack watertightly all items that can be damaged by water

This is important, because no rucksack is truly watertight, even though it may appear to be so. It is also better to pack each item separately in a small plastic bag (and the whole lot together in a larger bag) than to throw everything together in a large bag.

* Mark the different items

Marking is necessary especially if you are not using transparent plastic bags (in order to save a little, we usually use the yellow, orange and blue plastic bags of the large chain stores). In the case of meals, for example, we use yellow ones for breakfast, blue for lunch and the orange ones for supper. On each of these we indicate: breakfast day 1, lunch day 2, etc. The food for day 3 is packed right at the bottom of the rucksack while that of day 1 has to be readily accessible. The first-aid pack has to be marked clearly as well, and each separate unit in the pack has to be labelled clearly with medicines carrying clear dosage instructions — remember, it may happen that somebody else has to look for them in order to help you!

* Pack for carrying ease

It is important to pack the backpack so that it is balanced. Do not put all the heavy items in the side bags on the same side. More importantly, do not pack in such a way that it pulls your torso backwards. It is important to pack lighter items in the bottom, and the heavier items closer to the top and closer to your body.

* Pack in good time

Don't have any illusions — packing a backpack, especially if you are preparing for the whole family, is a big job. You have to measure and estimate repeatedly as you pack and repack. Thorough care and attention to this task will, however, assure a large measure of the success of the hiking trip. Allow plenty of time to get this done. Do not put it off until the last minute, because then chances are that you will forget something vital.

* Don't make it too heavy

Most inexperienced hikers tend to take along too many things and therefore have too much to carry. In the case of a family hike you have to be especially careful. Remember what I said: An adult should, if possible, carry no more than a third of his or her body weight, and children no more than a fifth. If you pack your backpacks at home, you can weigh them to make sure that they conform to the optimum weight. If you plan to pack at camp, take along a small spring balance.

Your gear can be divided into seven groups: clothes; toiletries; first-aid box; cooking and eating utensils; food; tent and sleeping gear; and, finally, the remainder. (For more details, see sections 3.4: *How to pack your backpack* and 3.5: *Checklist*.)

Clothes

This includes all the clothes which you and your family are not already wearing for a hike in good weather conditions, as well as the extra clean clothes which you may need for a hike over a few days.

I give the check-list so that you can check whether you have everything:
* rainsuit (and windbreaker)
* track suit (for the cold and to sleep in)
* warm sweater (not necessary if you are taking a track-suit)

* balaclava or woollen cap, woollen scarf, swimsuit, gloves (for women and small children)
* comfortable light shoes, such as tennis shoes, to wear after the day's hike or if your hiking boots get wet or break
* extra T-shirts, outer and underwear, socks and handkerchiefs.
* Your baby's additional needs will have to be taken care of.

Toiletries

This really includes the standard stuff that you need at home:
* a small bar of soap, facecloth, small towel, small tube of toothpaste and toothbrush (some hikers even cut off the handle of the tootbrush to cut down on weight!)
* shaving equipment
* deodorant
* face cream
* perfume and lipstick for women
* items for your specific personal needs.

Apart from the toilet roll that dad packs, each hiker should have small rolls of toilet paper wrapped in plastic cling wrap in his or her own rucksack.

When you hike with a baby, you will of course need additional items, like baby powder and cloths and cream needed for nappy changes.

First-aid kit

If you are unsure of what to take along, your doctor or pharmacist should be able to provide advice and prescriptions. It is important, however, to set up a first-aid kit specifically for hiking.

Special provision has to be made for specific areas, such as malaria tablets for the Lowveld and water purification tablets for areas where river water may not be clean.

Also pack supplies to treat blisters on your feet, insect bites, abrasions, blistered lips, sunburn, burns and allergies. Remember eardrops and eyedrops, salves or sprays for muscular pains, and never forget remedies for stomach upsets and headaches.

You may also need to take along a broad-spectrum antibiotic for children and adults.

I should like to offer a few suggestions about the use of the first-aid kit.

There are many opinions on remedies for blisters on the feet. Some people maintain that the blister should be left intact so that the skin can heal underneath, while others believe that the blister should be punctured and drained. I think the best idea is to prevent blisters. As soon as red chafing begins to show, cover it with sticking plaster and leave it on until the end of the trip (don't use the watertight type). Don't buy the pre-cut and pre-packed type of plaster. Rather get a roll which you can cut according to your needs. (Because I already know where I tend to get blisters, I now tend to stick plasters on before I even start out!)

There are many remedies for insect bites, and some of these help for more than one type of bite. At certain times of the year you can take along an insect repellent in order to prevent insect stings.

The best remedy for blistered and burst lips is still the old fashioned "lip ice". There are also many kinds of sunburn remedies. You can start taking sun tablets before setting out, but keep to the prescribed dosage. Also remember the possibility of serious and less serious burns through either an open flame or hot water.

Disinfectants, pain tablets, different kinds of bandages, eyedrops and eardrops, anti-allergic ointment, muscle rub, and plasters must obviously be included. Some people also tend to develop rubbing and chafing in uncomfortable spots, in which case nappy rash ointment is usually effective!

If either you or your children suffer from allergies, it is essential to take along antihistamines.

Should you be planning to hike in an area where the water in the streams may not be safe for drinking, you will have to take along water purification tablets which are obtainable at any shop selling hiking equipment, or at a pharmacy. You can, of course, also boil the water.

Your first-aid kit need not cost too much. It is really not necessary to go out and buy a lot of things, as most of these are items that you need at home anyway.

In the past I usually took an anti-snakebite kit along as part of my first-aid kit. Nowadays I feel safer leaving it at home because research has proved that more people have been adversely affected through the use of anti-venom than through the snakebite itself. Therefore snakebite serum is rarely administered today — even by doctors. Treatment is mostly symptomatic.

Snakes seldom attack. But if you or someone else is bitten by a snake, do not automatically assume that it is a venomous snake — the vast majority of snakes are quite harmless. Even if you are sure that a hiking companion has been bitten by a venomous snake, do not assume that he or she is in immediate danger. Keep him or her calm — panic could be more harmful than the bite itself. Do not suck or squeeze the bitten area and do not apply a tourniquet. Only clean the wound of any excessive venom. If possible, avoid any physical exertion or move-ment of the limb. If necessary, the victim may walk, but should not run. Get the person to the hospital as quickly as possible or summon medical aid — preferably within six hours. If respiratory difficulties occur before medical assistance is acquired, apply mouth-to-mouth resuscitation.

Cooking and eating utensils, and other hardware

The traditional way of cooking out in the open, over a wood fire, unfortunately is no longer possible because of the danger of bush fires and because wood is often not available.

The hiking family can, instead, choose from a whole range of stoves.

In the first place there are the solid-fuel stoves. They are cheap (around R30) and easy to handle, but experts say that they do not generate enough heat to cook for a whole family, and this prolongs the process of getting ready a meal for a tired family.

There is also a whole range of stoves which work with liquid fuel (paraffin, benzine or petrol) under pressure. In some cases they have to be heated a little to obtain the necessary pressure, while others have a small pump to speed up things. These expensive stoves all cost between R200 and R400, besides the fuel, which you have to carry in a strong, unbreakable container with a tightly-closing stopper to ensure that the smell of fuel does not permeate your whole rucksack.

Then there are the well-known and much cheaper gas stoves, which work with liquid gas (butane or propane) in disposable cylinders. They are simple to handle (you obtain a flame immediately and you can regulate the flame) and they are safe. They are also not expensive: for between R60 and R80 you can buy the stove, and gas cylinders cost about R5 each. This type of stove burns cleanly so that it is not necessary to wash soot off the saucepan after each meal. The only problem is that at great heights above sea level and at very low temperatures they do not work as well as stoves that work with liquid fuel under pressure. Seeing that families do not normally hike under such conditions (best left to true mountaineers!) this need not be a problem. We hiked in fairly cold weather about 2 000 metres above sea level in the Drakensberg and did not experience any problems. It is advisable, however, for a family of six to put two stoves under the saucepan — mountain water is cold and takes a fair duration of time to come to the boil.

Do keep children away when you are cooking. Burns are never pleasant, least so in the veld. The base of the gas stove is small so that it is not stable at the best of times, especially not on uneven ground with a big saucepan on top! Don't forget to buy a collapsible plastic pedestal for it. You should also try to make a cooking shield with the aid of, for example, backpacks stacked in a V to the windward side of the stove.

You should, of course, take along a few extra gas cylinders.

In shops selling hiking equipment one finds all sorts of interesting cooking utensils, which can include an aluminium saucepan, a frying pan, two plates and two plastic mugs, and a loose handle which you can use to handle either the saucepan or the frying pan on the stove. Because all these things slot into each other, they take up little space.

The problem in the case of a family, though, is that these sets are usually intended for two people. Instead of buying two sets of these (which can cost up to R130 each) I would advise buying two large aluminium saucepans which fit into each other — at less than a quarter of the price. Don't buy saucepans with long handles — these get in the way when you pack. Buy the type with short, blunt handles and then buy a saucepan pincer (at about

R10). When you carry the saucepans, pack all the loose cooking and eating utensils into them, so that you don't waste any space. You can also tie them to the outside of the backpack, but then you have to see to it that they are properly fastened and do not bang against each other — that noise can become irritating after a while!

I have mentioned two saucepans (a big one and a smaller one fitting inside it to save space) because that is the minimum on which our family of six can manage. If mother wants to make a second dish, soup or coffee, the second saucepan is indispensable. You can also use one of the saucepans as a frying pan.

One knife and fork for each person is enough, and everybody will need one spoon, seeing that you can deal with most dishes that way! (If you have extra money to spend you can buy durable plastic cutlery sets at about R15-R20 per set.)

Plastic cups and mugs are sometimes lighter than enamel mugs, but coffee does not really taste as good in a plastic mug. Most supermarkets carry a variety of plastic and enamel mugs.

I have almost forgotten to mention the plates — probably because we never take any along! As porcelain plates and even plastic plates are quite heavy and difficult to pack, we use aluminium-foil containers as plates. We buy the oval type that is slightly deeper that the aluminium pie dish, so that it can serve as a porridge plate and an ordinary plate. These containers are light and small, fit snugly into each other, and can be used over and over again. They are just right to boil a quick cup of water over the gas stove.

Should you decide to carry tinned food, remember the tin opener!

Matches have to be wrapped in cling film seeing that they easily become wet and are then totally useless. A cheap, disposable lighter is also a good friend on a trip.

Strictly speaking, water bottles are not cooking utensils, but they *are* hardware! Each member of the family must have one. A good one-litre bottle made of hard plastic (like the bottles used by the Defence Force) with a tight lid, a canvas cover and a shoulder strap costs about R25-R30.

Seeing that one needs a lot of water to cook dehydrated foods — quite apart from drinking water and to make tea, coffee, Milo and soup — six one-litre water bottles do not offer enough water to cook for a family of six. That is why we take along a few extra plastic bottles to carry water drawn from a stream. (You can use a plastic fruit-juice container or something of that sort.) This prevents a lot of unnecessary walking to and from the water source! Of course you don't pack such a large bottle in your rucksack, because it would take too much room. Tie the (empty) bottle to your backpack with a piece of string. A family with no financial restrictions may prefer to buy a collapsible five-litre pail from the hiking store (at about R25).

You should also pack a (plastic or copper) pot scourer, a piece of dishwashing soap (we use a well-known brand and we cut the stone into 2 cm X 2 cm pieces), and paper cloths to clean your dishes. If you forget the scourer and the soap you may find a handful of sand and grass almost as effective.

Parents must not leave behind the utensils to which baby is accustomed. The whole hiking experience will already be strange for your baby, and he should not be bereft of a trusted and well-known bowl and spoon!

Life in the dark can be most unsettling. We used to carry a gas lamp with us (it fits the same gas bottles as the stoves and it costs about R130). This takes up a lot of space, has to be packed carefully so that the glass doesn't

71

break, and the glow mantle does not last long in a bouncing backpack. Mom also worries constantly that one of the children will kick over the lamp in the tent. Nowadays, we take to our beds when it gets dark, while each member of the family has a small torch. These take little space, run on the smallest (penlight) batteries and only cost about R10,00 each at ordinary chain stores.

Food for the trail

This is an important element in your packing. I cannot possibly in the limited scope of this book include recipes. Here are a few general remarks, though, for the benefit of the uninitiated.

*	It is important that mother should carefully measure out (perhaps even weigh out) each day's provisions, so that you take neither too little nor too much. This is only possible if you have experimented a little at home, or after a few days spent on a hiking trail.

*	It is also essential to pack each day's meals in separate plastic bags. (You therefore plan veld menus in advance.) This will prevent a great deal of hunting around on the trail and also ensures that the children — who develop monstrous appetites out on the trail — do not devour all the stores in the first two days of a four-day trip! My wife even packs the coffee, tea, Milo and sugar, together with the salt and pepper — and even the piece of pot scourer and soap — into each day's container. Add a box of matches to each breakfast and supper! In this way you will have everything you need for a meal to hand, and will not need to break open other packs to remove just one item.

Each meal should be carefully labelled as breakfast 1, lunch 2 or supper 3. If you use plastic bags of different colour for the different meals, you will make things even easier. We use elastic bands to close up the bags rather than those twists that come with the plastic bags, because the twists tend to puncture the bags.

* Avoid all tinned food, unless one of the children is totally addicted to condensed milk or Vienna sausages in brine — and is willing to carry it himself! Anything that comes in dehydrated form is preferable to canned food. In this way you can easily cut more than 50% of the weight!

* For most hiking equipment you will find a sports goods or hiking store indispensable, but in the case of food you should avoid such stores. You can find practically everything you need much more cheaply in an ordinary supermarket or grocery store.

* For breakfast we usually eat an energy cereal, a piece of dried wors or biltong and we drink coffee or Milo. At lunch-times we try not to use the stove except when it is very cold, when soup is welcome. Foodstuffs that don't need cooking save a lot of time when one is out on the trail. In hot weather we therefore drink something cold rather than tea or coffee. Supper is the main meal, on which we spend a fair amount of time and trouble.

* Although I have suggested that you do not lug around too much food, it is also essential to take emergency rations covering one or two meals. One may be forced by bad weather or by an accident to remain out on the trail longer than planned, and then this is essential.

    Again, it is cheaper to put together your emergency rations yourself rather than buy it from a hiking shop.

* The sweet and salt snacks and cold-drink powder

that children crave between meals should also be carefully portioned out. The sweet things especially tend to run out quickly! Each day's store should therefore be placed in a separate, marked plastic bag.

* A recent calculation of the cost of hiking meals for our family came to about R12-R15 per person per day. This is only possible, of course, if you do not indulge in expensive items.

Breakfast options

Energy serials, wheat cakes or muesli (which you can mix yourself), with hot milk (made from powdered milk) plus a spoonful of sugar over the cereal (and later one or two in tea or coffee) will provide you with the energy you need. You can also, for the sake of variety, cook a little oatmeal (but then you have to clean the pot!). Eggs can be taken along whole or in liquid form in a plastic bottle (only sufficient for a day or so) and cooked for breakfast. (Our children don't like the powdered eggs which are available nowadays.) You can also serve a little biltong or dried wors. A mug of tea, coffee or malt drink will round off this humble breakfast — with perhaps a dried apple, prune, pear or banana.

Lunch options

You can carry along fresh bread or rolls, but these are quite heavy and take up a lot of room. Hard rye bread, matzos (unleavened dried bread) and salt biscuits can be used instead. "Dog biscuits" (army issue) can be found in hiking shops and "liga" biscuits are nutritious and popular with the kids.

Because butter and margarine melt so easily it is advisable to take along processed cheese in various forms of packaging, such as wedges and rolls, to eat with the bread or bread substitute. Peanut butter mixed with syrup on a slice of brown bread is sheer bliss.

Meat can be carried in the form of biltong or dried wors, salami, or dried, smoked garlic sausages. In cold weather everyone is given a mug of hot soup.

This can be followed by a handful of nuts and perhaps a slice of dried banana. The meal can be rounded off with **aqua pura** (water from a cold mountain stream) or a mug of isotonic cold drink (from a powder satchel). The children always welcome a sweet, such as a piece of candy or chewing gum.

Supper options

For starters a mug of instant soup will quell the harshest hunger pangs. Mom and dad can have a quiet sherry, or fetch the can of beer — carried with great sacrifice all the way — from the cool mountain stream.

For the main dish, spiced soybean mince can be served with powdered potato mash or instant noodles. Some soybean dishes are heavily spiced, and it may be a good idea to try them out on the children at home first. (Carefully read the instructions on the packages.)

Another popular dish in our family is soybean "meat" with a good portion of dehydrated vegetables. An onion which is dug up from the depths of dad's rucksack, fried in a little cooking oil carried along in a small bottle, whets all the appetites. This dish is then served on spaghetti and topped off with pieces of cheese or cheese powder.

For dessert you can mix an instant pudding. Or, if mom is not too tired, stewed dried fruit and instant custard is always a hit.

A last warm drink with perhaps a home-made rusk before bedtime will make everybody sleep like a baby.

Well, there you have a start. Perhaps each hiker's meals are the single most individual aspect of the whole hiking experience, and for that reason I have only offered some suggestions for the real rookies among you.

You will note that I have not mentioned the babies. They have to be fed their normal meals like milk (from powder), porridge and bottled foods out on the trail, which entails making special provision for them.

Living and sleeping gear

I have mentioned that we sleep in track suits when it's cold, or in the next day's clean T-shirt when it's hot.

Here are some brief suggestions regarding the tent, ground-sheet, foam mattress, sleeping bag, pillow and the possible use of a space blanket.

These articles are usually carried attached to the outside of the rucksack. The tent, with posts and pegs (in strong separate bags in the tent bag, so that they can't puncture the tent) can be rolled up in the foam mattress to protect it against damage by branches and stones. The sleeping bag is rolled up tightly and put into a plastic garbage bag with the pillow before being wrapped in the groundsheet and attached to the backpack. You already know that the heavier things, such as the tent with attachments, should be at the top of the backpack and the lighter things, such as sleeping equipment, at the bottom.

Rope can't always be tightened sufficiently; it tends to cut into soft materials, and untying the knot is often a problem. Nowadays we have nylon straps with buckles that enable us to tighten and loosen things quickly.

Hikers' tents

These are available in various shapes and sizes, accommodating between two and six people. Depending on the size, quality and trademark, the prices can vary from around R400 to about R2 000! (If you plan to hike along a trail with overnight huts, this will obviously not be an issue.)

It is important to note that your tent should be as light as possible, easy to pitch, large enought for all the members of the family and good enough to withstand rain and wind. If your party includes grandparents, perhaps they will prefer a separate two-man tent.

Hiking tents nowadays are made of polyurethane covered nylon. This material is watertight against rain and dew, but condensation inside the tent cannot escape. As soon as the damp reaches the roof of the tent, it condenses. On a cold, rainy day you can get as wet inside the tent as outside it, and this is no exaggeration! During the night — and nights on the trail can be twelve hours long — the average adult expirates about half a litre of fluid. This means that a mother, father and two children sharing a tent can be soaked by one and a half litres of water. The problem has to some extent been overcome by the double roof, with outside walls of nylon doctored with polyurethane, but the inner roof consisting of nylon doctored with silicone. The silicone lets through the interior moisture, this condenses on the flysheet, and the drops fall onto the inner roof, but run down to the ground because of the silicone. (A wonderful material has been on the market for some time now. It is called gore-tex and it "replaces" the functions of a double layer. It is ideal for rain coats where a similar condensation problem is encountered.)

In passing: The condensation problem inside a tent is well regulated if the windows are kept open throughout the night. The tent is not primarily intended to keep the air warm but to protect you against rain and wind. Your clothes have to provide the warmth — and one is out in nature specifically to enjoy the benefits of fresh air, after all.

If you buy a tent, ask the trader to pitch it for you and check whether the division between the inner and outer roofs is big enough so that wind or strong rain won't compress it and destroy the watertightness.

You also have to check that the floor (usually of sturdy watertight material) does not have unwelded seams. The floor-sheet section must not only cover the floor, it should extend up the wall sides for a few centimetres. This prevents running ground water from the sides getting into the tent and turning it into an indoor swimming pool!

Also check whether the zips of the windows and the door are made of durable plastic. The window openings are usually also covered with nylon gauze, so that the window flaps can be left open without fear that one will be pestered by insects.

The tent posts and pegs should be made of aluminium to keep the weight as low as possible. Always take a few extra pegs, ropes and elastic bands if the tent is provided with those. They are easy to lose or break, and in stormy weather you may need them to keep the tent secured.

A few hints on pitching the tent: Practise on the lawn at home so that you can do this rapidly and easily. Also try to do it in the dark, rain and wind — this may become necessary out on the trail!

When you are pitching your tent on the trail, try to find a space that is not too uneven and not too far away from water. If you can't find such a place pitch it in such a way that you can lie with your feet lower than your head and not vice versa.

Also scour the terrain to remove all pebbles, sticks and other sharp objects to prevent disturbed sleep and punctured tent floors. You should never tramp about in hiking boots on the floor of the tent .

It is also not advisable to pitch the tent under a tree. It

is especially dangerous to settle in a hollow or on the bank of a river. In a mountainous region a low-lying site or the smooth bank of a stream can become a seething river which takes everything in its tow — and this can include the whole family! You can never tell. There may have been a rainstorm higher up in the mountains of which you may not even be aware. Some years ago three young people died in the Drakensberg in such circumstances.

We prefer cooking outside the tent, because of the danger of fire, steam condensation, and the possibility of soiling the tent floor. These problems are intensified when there are children inside the tent. In rainy and stormy weather, of course, there is no choice.

A final thought about using the tent. The space between the roof and the inner walls of the tent offers useful overnight storage for cooking utensils and other items. We stack other valuable articles, like the first-aid kit and extra dry clothes, at the children's feet. The backpacks we leave outside, because there is no space for them inside our two tents and also because their frames can easily puncture the tents. To protect the backpacks and their contents, we store them in sturdy plastic bags (the so-called survival bags) and stack a few stones on top, so that they cannot be blown away.

The bedding

If you want an extra ground-sheet on the floor of the tent, you can also use thick survival bags (about R15) for this purpose. An 8 - 10 mm thick foam mattress, with sealed surfaces so that it does not absorb water like "open" foam does, is adequate. They cost about R35 each.

Sleeping bags are available in a large variety of trademarks, quality, shapes and prices. Sleeping bags filled with (hollow) synthetic fibre are available from about R200 - R400. Down sleeping bags are expensive — between R300 and R 1 000 each.

A down sleeping bag is, of course, the best buy. It is light, retains heat and can be rolled up compactly. It does have disadvantages, though. The biggest problem is that it loses its insulatory quality when it becomes wet, and it does not dry out quickly. Also, make sure that none of the members of the family is allergic to down!

Keep your down sleeping bag clean inside and outside. It should not be washed too often, and then only in accordance with definite specifications, including special soap. You can line it on the inside with a special sheet or lining to keep it clean. If you have babies who still wet their beds at night, I would really recommend a waterproof lining between the baby and the sleeping bag.

Little ones sleep warmly in a sleeping bag with mom or dad — but then the bags should be large enough, or they must be the type that zip open completely and zip onto another one to form a double sleeping bag.

All you still need is a pillow. You can buy an inflatable pillow, or simply use the inside (bladder) of an empty 5-litre wine cask! My wife made us special foam pillows which fit snugly into a tiny space in the backpack. Before this we simply used a pile of clothes as a headrest!

You may think it insane to sleep so primitively, but I can assure you that you will soon become used to this, and when you get back home a soft bed will feel distinctly funny!

A further word to those who easily feel the cold and long for their electric or woollen blanket. Space blankets, available in shops at around R100 each, offer extra help. They can be used to cover you or to insulate your body from the ground underneath, and with the shiny side turned towards you they will reflect most body heat back and keep you wonderfully warm.

This type of blanket works like a thermos flask, and can be used to keep heat either in or out. On a hot day, when the temperature inside the tent is particularly unbearable, you can fasten a space blanket on to the roof, shiny side out. Space blankets which are not so strong and only cost about R10, are available for emergencies. They fold up small enough to fit into one hand.

Remember the balaclava or woollen cap to keep your head warm, and see to it that there is a flashlight handy. Ensure especially that you know how to find the flashlight in darkness when a child should have a nightmare.

A useful night toilet can be made from a coffee tin or a large plastic bottle with a tight-fitting lid. If you have this handy, the younger children need not be scared that they might step on a snake when going out in the middle of the night.

I have never slept badly out in the open. The exercise and the fresh air are conducive to deep and refreshing sleep, which I am sure your family will also experience.

Other items

Essentials

A number of extra **plastic bags** of different sizes should always go along. This includes garbage bags for water-tight packing of sleeping bags and other large items. Extra bags are essential because they tear so easily.

I also carry a small **tool kit.** This contains at least the following: a pocket knife, small pliers, a piece of wire (to make emergency repairs to, for excample, backpacks), extra clevis pins, a piece of nylon rope, insulation tape, a tube of seam sealer for the tent, a few extra shoelaces, needle and thread.

Apart from this I carry my **maps, permits, pocket Bible, a notebook** and **a pencil.**

I have already mentioned small **flashlights** for the whole family. Remember to take extra **batteries**. Turn the batteries in the flashlight during the day so that two negatives or two positives press against each other. This will discourage the children from playing with the light all the time and will also prevent them from accidentally switching on during the hike.

A **whistle** for each member of the family is useful, but this should not have the effect of making you relax too much and think that your child can't get lost. You cannot hear a whistle far against the wind or in uneven mountainous terrain.

For hiking with a family some card or board **games** (lightweight and easy to carry) are indispensable. This can be a magnetic chessboard and decks of cards. When the family is stranded in the tent by rain or snow or over a long night you must have something to keep the children occupied.

Don't forget **change**, to make a phone call or for a promised cold drink in case you pass a farm shop. Fasten your **car keys** to the inside of the backpack with a piece of string so that you don't lose them or have to hunt for them endlessly when they are required.

I have almost forgotten my faithful companion. I would like to recommend it to you: a **walking stick**. It is not an expensive item of heavy wood either — I bought it at the local agricultural co-op from the shelf containing broomsticks. It has helped me up and down inclines and through rivers. It can also be used for a variety of other purposes, such as to prop up a rucksack, as an extra tent pole and — if you have two of them — as a stretcher pole or a splint in the case of an accident. You can also carve notches in it for each hiking kilometre or ten which you cover!

Non-essentials

There are other accessories which are not direly needed, but they can make the hike interesting and informative.

* A **camera** (or cameras) and extra film is a non-essential, because not everybody is mad about photography. But for me it is essential. You can double the enjoyment of a hiking trip if you take out the photographs or slides again later to relive the experience. You can also use the hiking trip as an opportunity to teach a child to use the camera.
* If you go on a hike in a completely uncharted area, you will need a **compass.** We usually take it along anyway (a cheap one does not cost more than some R40), because the children like working out the directions with it.
* Another interesting — but more expensive — piece of apparatus is a **pedometer** (at around R70) and an **altimeter** (much more expensive, at about R175). The pedometer has the advantage that it gives you new courage when you can see that, in spite of the slow pace, you have already covered some kilometres, or you can see how many are left. (On national hiking trails where there are distance indicators this is, of course, not necessary.)
* **Binoculars** (from R300-R5 000) are useful, because you can look at the landscape, watch birds and animals and at night watch the stars, using the opportunity to teach the children something about astronomy.
* A **small pocket radio** (about R150) maintains contact with civilization and offers cheerful music in the evening. It can also be important if you should need to listen to the weather forecast.
* **Field guides** (books about birds, mammals, butterflies, etc.) should not be too heavy to carry. Books are

easily damaged during a trip. It is probably better if the family does advance reading at home. A good idea is to concentrate on one aspect during a specific trip — birds this time round, and flowers the next round — so that you need carry only one manual per trip.

* Many hikers prefer to stay away from a **mirror** during a trip. Apart from the fact that shaving (if you intend doing it!) is easier with a mirror, it can also be used to signal during an emergency. Of course, you need not carry a glass mirror which can break easily. Stainless steel mirrors are cheap (only about R10).

3.4 HOW TO PACK YOUR BACKPACK

On the diagram the different compartments of a regular backpack are indicated by numbers. The following list indicates how items may be packed. (For details see below, 3.5: CHECKLIST.) Also refer to the general packing hints under 3.3 above, e.g. to pack in such a way that the backpack is balanced. The lighter items should be packed at the bottom and the heavier ones closer to the top and closer to your body.

1. Fastened to the frame of backpack
Tent, poles and pegs.

2. Top compartment
Raincoat, sun-hat, balaclava, gloves, pots, dishes, knife, fork, spoon, etc. Food for the first day.

3. Map pocket
Map, notebook, pencil, permit(s), identification document(s), field guide(s), pocket money, car keys.

4. Middle and lower compartment
Food (on top) and clothing (below).

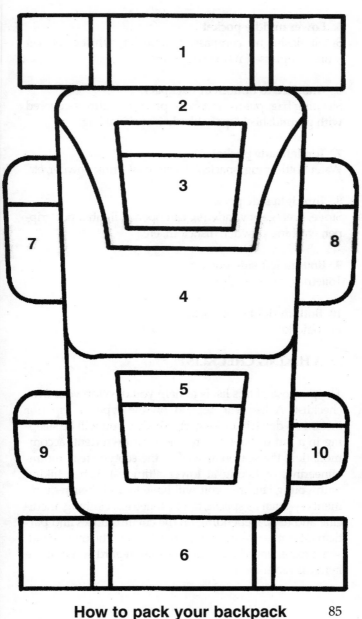

How to pack your backpack

5. Lower middle pocket
Small flashlight, compass, pedometer, whistle, pocket knife, sunglasses, nylon straps, etc.

6. Attached to bottom of backpack
Sleeping bag, pillow and foam pad/air mattress covered with groundsheet/space blanket/survival bag.

7. Top left side pocket
Water bottle, mug, snacks/sweets, cool-drink powder, etc.

8. Top right side pocket
Stove, fuel/gas cylinder(s), can opener, lighter, pot gripper, washing powder, dishcloth, etc.

9. Bottom left side pocket
Toiletries, camera, film(s)

10. Bottom right side pocket
First-aid kit.

3.5 A HIKING CHECKLIST

The purpose of this list is to help you develop your own checklist. A list will depend on the type of trip (for instance a day trip or longer), whether you will be sleeping in a hut or have to provide your own (tent) accommodation, the season as well as the ecotype (e.g. mountaineering, or hiking at lower altitudes). When hiking with young children you will have to add their requirements — such as special foods, toiletries, clothing, medicine and toys. Depending on the circumstances and participants, other items may be needed. On the other hand, some experienced backpackers may regard some of the items as redundant.

CLOTHING

Boots ☐
Spare footwear/sandals ☐
Shirts/T-shirts ☐
Shorts/Slacks (long pants) ☐
Underwear ☐
Socks ☐
Sun-hat ☐
Track suit ☐
Cardigan/woollen sweater/windbreaker ☐
Balaclava (woollen hat) ☐
Mittens/gloves ☐
Scarf ☐
Handkerchiefs ☐
Gaiters (for vegetation or wet weather) ☐
Swimming costume ☐
Waterproof raincoat/poncho ☐

TOILETRIES

Toilet towel ☐
Toilet paper ☐
Towel ☐
Facecloth ☐
Soap ☐
Toothbrush plus toothpaste ☐
Shaving kit ☐
Mirror ☐
Comb or hairbrush ☐
Sun-screen cream ☐
Insect repellent ☐
Moisturising cream ☐
Lip salve ☐
Foot powder ☐
Deodorant ☐
Cosmetics ☐

FIRST-AID KIT

First-aid manual ☐
Small knife/scissors ☐
Tweezers ☐
Candle/small flashlight ☐
Lighter/matches ☐
Safety pins ☐

Adhesive first-aid tape ☐
Gauze, eye and other bandages ☐
Salt tablets (if isotonic drinks are not allowed
or available) ☐
Sun tablets ☐
Pain killer(s) ☐
Malaria pills (if applicable) ☐
Antihistamines (for insect bites) ☐
Different ointments/salves for nappy rash, muscular pains
(topical analgesics) wounds (antiseptic) and burns ☐
Eye- and eardrops ☐
Anti-diarrhoea and anti-nausea tablets ☐
Water purification tablets ☐
Broad-spectrum antibiotics ☐
Medicine for the treatment of blisters and chafing ☐
Personal medication ☐

COOKING AND EATING UTENSILS

Pots ☐
Pot gripper ☐
Camp stove ☐
Extra fuel or gas cylinders ☐
Fuel container ☐
Water bottles ☐
Matches/lighter ☐
Can opener ☐
Dishes ☐
Knife, fork, spoon ☐
Mug/cup ☐
Washing-up powder/soap (biodegradable) ☐
Scouring pad ☐
Dishcloth ☐
Plastic refuse bags ☐

FOODS

I give no specific check-list for food (fresh, dried, canned, dehydrated or freeze-dried) or drinks (tea, coffee, Milo, isotonic powder and milk powder) because this depends on personal taste. Remember, however, always to take along emergency rations (high energy).

FOR CAMPING AND SLEEPING

Backpack ☐
Tent with poles, pegs and extra nylon rope ☐
Sleeping bag ☐
Closed-cell foam pad or air mattress ☐
Ground sheet ☐
Space blanket (for very cold or hot weather) ☐
(Inflatable) pillow ☐
Gas lamp or flashlight ☐
Survival bag (optional) ☐

MISCELLANEOUS (other essential and non-essential items)

Permits ☐
Personal identification (ID document or passport), visas ☐
Map(s) ☐
Trail guide/brochure/field guide(s) ☐
Walking stick ☐
Binoculars ☐
Camera and film ☐
Notebook/paper and pen/pencil ☐
Fishing equipment ☐
Pedometer, altimeter, compass ☐
Whistle ☐
Pocket knife ☐
Pocket money ☐
Motor car keys ☐
Needle and thread ☐
Small pliers and wire ☐
Extra nylon straps/rope ☐
Spare batteries ☐
Spare spectacles/sunglasses ☐
Waterproof plastic bags ☐
Umbrella ☐

4. THE HIKING EXPERIENCE

A three-day family hiking trip in the Drakensberg from Injasuti Hutted Camp to Monks Cowl Campsite.

As stated at the outset, the concept of backpacking has three elements: the hiker, his pack and the activity itself. We have already seen the preparations that go into the trip, and we have seen what has to go into the pack. Now for the climax, the hiking experience itself. The crucial moment has arrived . . .

You are as ready as you are ever going to be for hiking with your backpack on your back, and the children are dancing around, impatiently chanting: "Let's go! Mom and Dad, come on!"

The theory on hikers and the packs they carry has limitations, for hiking itself has to be experienced. No book can ever deal with every aspect and answer all questions.

The best schooling for hiking is not sitting at home reading a manual, but getting out on the trail and walking! You should not know it all before you start out — there should be an element of surprise, problems upon which you unexpectedly stumble, even chances to try, and then to make mistakes . . . This is part of the challenge and part of the pleasure of hiking. Mostly these are the experiences the family will most often remember and talk about in time to come.

I am going to take you along in retrospect on a three-day hike that we had as a family; presenting events as if you are, as it were, watching a film.

The intention is to whet your appetite for that hiking trip which your family anticipates . . .

4.1 Arrival at Monks Cowl

Dave and Margie Osborne look at us incredulously when

we arrive, as if we have just dropped in from a strange planet.

"Morning! We did not expect you!"

"Yes, I know we said we were not coming, but on Saturday, when we finished painting the house, we decided to come after all. You should know better than anyone that once a person has fallen in love with the mountains it is impossible to stay away for longer than six months." So Mom explains charmingly.

"Come in, come in! It is just time for tea. Let's hear how you all are."

How wonderful to know these friendly people! We have been cordially received by these people so often that it feels like coming home to family.

A new route

Once all the family news of the last six months is shared, Dad can test his hiking plans on Dave. "We should like to reach Champagne Castle via Grey's Pass, or to hike up to Injasuti from here. What route would you recommend, Dave?"

Dad and the boys are not quite so taken with Dave's recommendation. He recommends the route to Solitude. After take-over by the Natal Parks Board it has been renamed Injasuti Camp, but our menfolk see the 3 377 metre-high Champagne Castle as a challenge which has to be overcome. We had hoped to break a champagne bottle right on its pinnacle, but Mom is visibly relieved at Dave's advice.

The urge to reach the top of Champagne Castle is visible in Dad's eyes, and it is not going to die. Dad has promised during the journey here that if Champagne Castle is not scaled this time round, it will be done in December, when we will come here with four other

Potchefstroom families. There will be four strong men and at least two sturdy boys to face the challenge. Doctor Andre, Uncle Bert and Uncle Fanie have all expressed enthusiasm for such an adventure.

Dave breaks the silence when he sees that not everybody is equally happy with his recommendation. "To hike from here to Injasuti is a lovely experience. Few people do the route, and if you take three days you can do it at a comfortable pace. I am sure that you will enjoy it."

"How far is it, Uncle?" Mias asks.

"We can measure it on the topographic map with the dividers, but I estimate it to be about 30 kilometres."

We say goodbye for the time being as another visitor arrives and we still have to pitch our tents.

New drama in the Drakensberg

Dad knows that many dramatic things happen in the Drakensberg that one does not read about in the papers or journals and does not see on television. He relies on Margie and Dave to keep us in the picture. That becomes the topic when we walk over to their home later on the same evening.

The young ones are usually enthralled by these exchanges.

"Didn't you have problems during the heavy snow last month?" Dad asks. The children move closer.

"Well, fortunately, nothing too serious. Two doctors, two nurses and a lawyer were snowed in on top of Champagne Castle. They just wanted to stay the one night, but when they got up in the morning, Grey's Pass had snowed in and they could not come down. They were stuck up there with just enough food for one day."

"What happened?"

"Well, when the snow had not melted after three days, they were brought down by helicopter. They had to ration their food carefully, but apart from being very hungry, they were unharmed. Fortunately they were sensible people."

"Oh, I wish I could see a helicopter flying people out of the mountain," Barend says. Little does he know how soon his wish will be fulfilled.

The evening passes quickly. Dave informs us that he and other researchers are involved in photographing Drakensberg birds to publish in a book they are planning. He also shows us some wonderful slides. He may meet us at Injasuti, because he is going out to photograph a rare white stork nesting with little ones.

Before we leave, we schedule a braai together for the Friday evening. The next day (Tuesday) we intend driving out to Solitude and hiking from there. We hope to be back by Thursday evening, but decide that we will probably be too tired then to have a braai. For a completely different reason though, of which we are as yet totally unaware, it is just as well that we did not make a date for Thursday evening.

The Drakensberg was preparing for a new drama . . .

Spring, lovely spring!

This is only the second time the family has come here for the October holidays. Usually we come at the beginning of autumn, during the April holidays. For excellent weather, April-May is about the best time. Although it often rains during December, we have been here a few times. I remember the lovely veld flowers when we were here in October two years ago.

While we wait for the coffee-water to boil, we listen with great enjoyment to the wide variety of birdsong. The red-chested cuckoo (piet-my-vrou) sounds like a gramophone record that got stuck. He can't find his wife! There are also spotted-backed weavers, a malachite sunbird, two fork-tailed drongos and a southern bou-bou. Close to our tents a robin and a wagtail are hopping on the grass. Our familiar beaky old friends, **Bostrychia hagedash,** greet us with a raucous hak-hak-ha-de-da before they rush off to find breakfast.

Mias, the enthusiastic bird expert in our family, has quite forgotten about breakfast. Dad recently bought an audiovisual programme about South African birds from an oil company, which apart from a series of descriptive booklets also contains slides of the different birds and cassette tapes of their calls. Mias has clandestinely brought along the battery-powered cassette player, and is now playing the tape to try and determine whether he can identify any of the calls we are hearing. Perhaps he can lure wild birds with the calls from the tape player!

While the olive thrush on the branch sings its heart out, and the first sunlight shyly peeks over the mountain peaks, I realize what a celebration of life it is to be surrounded by such birdsong.

Back to reality

"Mias, have you done the dishes?" Mom's voice is pitched at a dangerous level. She does not know that Mias has not even eaten yet!

Dad barks so many orders simultaneously that confusion ensues. "Have you rolled your sleeping bags? Have you all got your boots on? Come and pile all your hats here, so that we don't forget them again. Barend and George, why haven't you filled the water bottles yet? Marieta, what did you do with the bus key? Mias, if you don't get away from those birds now and wash the dishes, you're in trouble. Have you all weighed your backpacks to make sure they're not too heavy? Don't come crying to me if you can't carry them!"

Well, this is nothing unusual for the start of a hike. It is like the confusion of Babel as commands and frantic searches follow in fast succession. The preparations for the hike are not my favourite part of the trip, I confess!

The drive to Solitude is interesting, though. We stop at Sooilaer, with its humble little monument where the Voortrekkers, during their travels in Natal, had pitched a laager alongside the Little Tugela River.

We also drive through an area where many Zulus still live in the round beehive huts which we have only seen before in paintings of Dingaan's kraal. We see a few women at work, building a hut. They make a sturdy framework of wood. The grass is then threaded onto the frame with ropes plaited from thinner grass.

Injasuti Camp lies deep in the mountains. There is not even a telephone. The old name "Solitude" was really suitable, because it is a truly isolated place, far away from civilization. We cross lovely streams with deep, quiet pools. Dad tells us that this is the source of the Tugela. The Cowl Fork, Ship's Prow Pass River, the Old Woman's Stream and the Injasuti all later converge into the Tugela River.

4.2 THE FIRST DAY OF THE HIKING TRIP

After buying a map of the area, locking the minibus and drinking belliesful of the clean mountain water from a tap, we swing the heavy backpacks on to our backs to begin the walk. The sky is clear, the air is fresh and energy levels high.

We soon reach a sign which indicates that we are entering the Mdedelelo Wilderness Area. "Mdedelelo" is the Zulu name for Cathkin Peak, and is best translated as "bully". Cathkin is the largest peak, and can presumably "bully" — subdue — all the peaks around it!

The wilderness must remain wild

"Dad, what is a wilderness area?" George asks when we sit down in the shade of a large rock to drink some isotonic cold drink.

"George, in simple language it is an area which the government has set aside to be preserved exactly as it is. Nobody can build anything on it or take anything out. Nature must remain untouched. Here you must only study and not disturb. A photograph and memories are all you may take away from here."

"Dad, but why should there be wilderness areas?" Marieta wants to know.

"My child, once you have lived in a city like Johannesburg you will understand this better. Even in our own town there is not much left of unspoilt nature. And people are part of nature. We can't really live without the soil, plants and animals."

"Dear, you will have to stop the nature conservation lesson for the time being," Mom interrupts. "We have been sitting here in the shade far too long."

Breathtaking vistas

The further we walk the more breathtaking are the views of Champagne Castle, Monks Cowl and Cathkin Peak. This is something special, because from the Monks Cowl Forestry Station it is not possible to see Monks Cowl properly, even though it rears up vertically dead straight for 3 234 metres.

We are still climbing. We are not quite used to the exercise and the hot sun . . . Fortunately we reach a shallow cave in one of the krantzes and Mom decides to call a halt for lunch.

On the trail Mom never needs to order: "Eat up all

your food!" Everybody attacks the food like a ravenous wolf. We have dry rye crisps with cheese, biltong, dried apples, peanuts and raisins.

"Barend, have you had enough?"

"No, Ma. I wouldn't quite say so!"

This is, of course, a broad hint for the little bit of sweetness we expect at the end of the meal. When everybody has had a piece of chocolate, water from the cool mountain stream below the cave rounds off lunch. Now we have a quarter of an hour long rest period.

About Bushmen and caves

But Dad is not allowed a chance to nap.

"Dad, are there many caves around here? I mean, really big ones?" George is already rested and always inquisitive.

"Look at the map. Read it aloud to all of us."

George reads, and we count the following names: Wonder Valley Caves, Grindstone Caves, Junction Cave, Lower Injasuti Cave, Fergy's Cave, Battle Cave and Poacher Stream Cave. There are quite a few more places where the little signs indicate the existence of caves which probably have not been named yet.

"Are there Bushmen drawings in these caves, like in the Ndedema Valley?"

"Yes, the Battle Cave has lovely drawings. Uncle Alex Wilcox told me about them."

"Who is Uncle Wilcox?" Marieta wants to know.

"This is the man who lives just round the corner from Uncle Reg Pearse. His farm is called 'Round the bend'. He is an expert on Bushmen art. He has written two books about rock art in Southern Africa."

"Will Dad again tell us about the Bushmen who lived here? I have almost forgotten what you told us about them in the Sabaaieni Cave next to the Ndedema River."

"Not now, Barend. We have to move on — the quarter of an hour of rest has become half an hour!"

Setling in for the night

The rest of the afternoon we spend slowly ascending Cataract Valley. We decide to stop no later than four o'clock to pitch camp for the night.

Everybody wants to check Dad's pedometer specially bought for the trip. "Only six and a half kilometres? Impossible!"

"I think the reading is right, though. Remember we were late starting out from Solitude, and we were going uphill all the time," Mom says consolingly.

The most suitable site we can find to overnight is on a fairly strong incline — with lots of large grass clumps. Well, it is not too damaging to the ecology to cut down dry grass. This gives Mias the opportunity to use his hunting knife, and George his new pocket knife. With four knives among us we "prune" the longer grasses.

Mom uses cut grass to fill up the hollows between the clumps, we spread two survival bags over the grassy mattress, and soon the blue tents are securely pitched. We don't know what our sleep will be like, as we have never slept against such a steep incline. We do know, however, that we won't sleep head downwards!

An appetite like a vulture . . .

How Mom manages it, we don't know, but with the help of only two small gas stoves and two saucepans we are soon tucking into a gourmet meal. She modestly says that hunger is the best cook — which is probably partly true, because the mountain air does wonders for our appetite. In springtime it can still be rather cold at night and we need a little extra fuel to generate body heat. Mom says that a male hiker needs about 12 500 kilojoules per day, and if he is climbing steep inclines in the cold, this can go up to about 21 000 kilojoules.

Just as a car needs water besides fuel, man also needs lots of fluids. It is very dangerous to become dehydrated, especially when you are walking with children who do not realize that they have to drink lots of water. You have to see to it that they get enough to drink. Fortunately there is no lack of lovely clear, cold streams here in the Drakensberg!

Evening devotions in the mountains

Instead of the small volume containing the New Testament and Psalms which we always carry with us, Dad takes out a few sheets of paper.

"What are you reading to us tonight, Dad?"

"From the Bible, of course!"

"But you haven't got a Bible there!"

"Well, on our previous trips I always used to read the beautiful Psalms (19, 29 and 104) about nature, but this time I wanted to read something else about nature. I chose Job chapters 37 to 40. As our small Bible contains only the New Testament and Psalms, I photocopied a few pages from Job before we left."

"That's a good idea. It saves us space and we don't damage our Bible," Mom says approvingly.

Dad tells the story of Job in broad outline, then he reads Job 37 and 38. In these chapters God directs Job's attention to the great miracles of nature: the snow, light, hail, lightning, wind, rain, ice and frost. Who made them?

God's intention with Job is to make him realize that He is great. We also see the mighty natural phenomena when we walk in nature. They make us realize that God is omnipotent.

During this hike we learn to sing a new hymn — Psalm 33. We already know the first and the last verses, but Dad has photocopied all the verses so that we can learn something extra every evening.

God spoke his word to make the heavens;
his spirit gave the stars their birth.
He gathers all the oceans' waters;
in storehouses around the earth.
Who should not adore Him,
stand in awe before Him?
What He spoke was done:
place and life were given
to seas, earth and heaven.
Let all fear the Lord!

A lesson in astronomy

"Dad, what does God mean when He mentions the beautiful Pleiades, and the Bear and the Cubs?"

"These are, of course, references to stars or galaxies. If I have to start telling you about stars we will be here all night, and you are all tired."

"Who's tired? Not us! Please, Daddy, please!" Dad has told us about a lot of things, but never about the stars.

There is no doubt that George has spoken on behalf of everybody, and Dad declares he'll tell if Mom makes more coffee.

"Perhaps I should first tell you about the universe, then about the earth, and then we can talk again about Orion, the Bear, the Pleiades and the zodiac.

"We live on a rather small planet (Earth) which rotates around a star of medium size, the Sun. The Earth is very small compared to the sun. The diameter of the earth is about 12 500 km and that of the Sun more than a million km. But the universe does not consist only of the Sun and the Earth. The Sun, together with about 100 000 million other stars, turns inside a huge galaxy, the Milky Way. And the Milky Way in turn is only one galaxy among innumerable others!

"We do not know whether there are limits to the universe. But to cross the section we know at the speed of light (299 300 km per second) would take 6 000 years, and man only lives for 70 or 80 years. Or, to take another example, if a rocket should travel through the Milky Way at 60 000 km per hour, crossing it would take 670 million years! To travel at the same speed between the Sun to the furthest planet, Pluto, would take only four and a half years.

"Another example of the enormous distances in space is the huge galaxy with the name Andromeda, which is comparable with our galaxy, the Milky Way. The group of stars in the constellation Andromeda is the furthest object in the universe which can be seen with the naked eye — but it is two million light years away from us!"

"What is a light year?" Barend asks.

"A light year is the distance that light travels in one year. I have told you how far it can travel in a second. Light travels at around 9,4 million km per year. If Andromeda is therefore two million light years from us, you can do the calculation — the answer would be the figure 18 with eighteen noughts added! For the sake of interest: The whole Milky Way is about 100 000 light years wide."

"That is amazing!" George says spontaneously. "In other words, there may be stars which we are not able to see because they are so far away that their light has not even reached us yet."

"Correct."

"Or there may be stars which you can see today, which might not even exist any more," Mias adds.

"Yes, and what we can see from the Earth are not the stars as they are, but as they were when the light rays which reach the Earth now, left them. For example, we always see the Sun as it was eight minutes before. The closest star to our galaxy, Proxima Centauri, is seen as it was four years ago."

"How many of the billions of stars can we see?" Mom wants to know.

"On a clear winter's night one can, with the naked eye, see about 2 000 to 2 500 stars. Binoculars would make visible thousands more. And with a good telescope one can see thousands of millions of stars."

Suddenly everybody scans the heavens. Mias takes out his binoculars and everybody gets a turn to look. The stars glitter in the heavens like precious jewels. We have watched the heavens often, but never with such a sense of wonder. There are bright ones and less bright ones. Some are so weak that one wonders whether it is a star or perhaps just imagination.

"Mom, watch this one for a moment. Is it my imagination or is it really a little reddish?"

It is Dad who helps with information which he recently found in an encyclopedia. "Stars do not all have the same shiny, white colour. There are yellow ones, red, orange, blue and white ones."

"But, Dad, you have not said anything about the zodiac and other things about which Job spoke." Barend never forgets a promise!

"Well the most important stars all have names, mostly Latin, Greek or Arabic. Many of them were named after animals, such as, for example, a bear, fish, lion, scorpion, etc. All these 'animal' stars together are called the zodiac. The Bear is one of them, and in reality there are two of them, the minor Bear and the major Bear. Each of the two Bears consists of seven stars. In the Northern Hemisphere this is a well-known, bright constellation, almost like the Southern Cross here. I doubt whether we should be able to see it in the Southern Hemisphere."

"But what about Orion and the Pleiades? Can Dad point them out?"

"Unfortunately, that is not possible, Marieta. Because the Earth rotates, one gets the impression that the stars — just like the Sun — move from east to west. All the stars are therefore not visible at all times. They also do not appear and disappear at the same time. Many people think that the skies are always the same. They have not looked properly; there are always changes.

"So far as I know, down here, one can only see Orion from January to April or May. Now, during October, we will not be able to see him. Orion's other name is the Hunter. It is not one star only, but a whole group. If one has a vivid imagination, one may draw imaginary lines between the stars of Orion, and see a hunter! Did you know that Orion is 1 000 light years away from us?"

"Can't we see the Seven Sisters?"

"The grand name for that star is the Pleiades. One can only see six stars with the naked eye, but with a telescope one can see that there are about 250 stars in this group, which is 300 light years from us. I know that one sees the seven (or six) sisters at about 9 o'clock on January 1 against the northern skies. I should think that they should also be visible tonight, but I don't know at what time and exactly where. I am really a novice when it comes to astronomy."

"Dad, won't you just point out one constellation

or star?" Mom tries to save the children disappointment.

Dad is able to point out the Southern Cross, but only once Barend has taken out the compass to find south!

"You can see that one can clearly see the Southern Cross (the learned name in Latin is **Crux**) with its four stars. This constellation is also not visible in the same place all of the time. From January to May it lies more westerly and from July until around November it clearly is more easterly. From October to January it is far more southerly, while during the other months at the same time of the day, it is much more northerly.

"Did you know that another star, the evening star, which is usually the first to be seen at night, is also the morning star? It was named after Venus, the Greek goddess of beauty, because apart from the sun and the moon, it is most clearly visible."

"Dad, what purpose does it serve to know about the stars?" Barend wants to know.

"Well, before people had good maps and there were no compasses at all, they had to determine their position at night by referring to the stars. The Southern Cross for example, clearly indicates south. To us, today, it is just a matter of interest."

"And now, you lot, it is really bedtime!"

Poor Mom can't stay awake any longer — never mind stargazing!

4.3 THE SECOND DAY OF THE TRIP

Dad seems to have decided to wake us up with a beautiful song every morning of the trip. He is whistling **Kumbaya:**

"Kumbaya, my Lord, Kumbaya

Kumbaya, my Lord, Kumbaya
Kumbaya, my Lord, Kumbaya
Oh, Lord, Kumbaya
Someone's crying, my Lord . . .
Someone's praying, my Lord . . .
Someone's singing, my Lord . . ."

At first, one is not really in the mood to join in early in the morning, but when Dad persists we start inside the tents, and we contribute the chorus!

Dad does not tell us anything about the surprise awaiting us outside. When we crawl out of the sleeping bags and the tents, stretching our stiff limbs, we see it: Our backpacks and tents are covered in white frost, and the water in the water bottles has frozen. We would never have thought that it can be so cold in the mountains at the beginning of October. We would definitely have frozen on Champagne Castle if we had decided to do that route!

An hour later we have had breakfast, rolled up the ·(slightly damp) tents and packed the rucksacks.

A feast for the eye — and the heart

This soon becomes one of the loveliest days we have ever spent in the Drakensberg. First we ascend quite some distance into the Cataract Valley. Then we join the long contour road which runs (at about 2 000 metres above sea level) practically from Giant's Castle in the south to Cathedral Peak in the north. It is a road full of ups and downs, and we pass through at least five branches of the Cowl Fork River. Each time we go down a steep incline and then up again, higher and higher. The valleys of the little rivers we pass are often densely wooded, and there is a lot of undergrowth or chinchibush, as the Zulus call it. But once we reach the top, the vistas in front of us are indescribable.

We see the high peaks of Champagne Castle, Monks Cowl and Cathkin. The view over the deep valleys is something that cannot be put into words. Dad's camera works overtime in order to try and capture something of this beauty for later. Each of the children is allowed to take four photographs with Dad's camera, and we have free choice of what we want to take.

Among the loveliest views are the pristine patches of pure white snow to the south of the high peaks. This we have never seen before.

And all around one's feet the feast of spring continues. Notwithstanding the fact that we have already seen so many spring flowers, we are stopped in our tracks in admiration. It is worth coming to the Drakensberg in October just to see the pink heather or ericas.

Danger lurks on the trail too . . .

But there are also dangers lurking around our feet. We come across no less than three snakes in a few hours — Dad walking right over one snake and Barend almost stepping onto another one. They are all brownish — probably mountain vipers — but they are gone so quickly that there is no time to identify them. In spite of Mom's injunction to wear long pants, Mias and George knew better this morning, but they are quick to unpack the slacks now!

When we stop for cold drinks, Mom notices two ticks — one on her leg and one on her sleeve.

"Check right away whether you have one of the beasties on you," she orders everybody. She has had tick-bite fever before, and she knows that the symptoms are most unpleasant. And what do we find? No fewer than three of our group have "picked up" unwelcome passengers! It may be true that only one tick out of every one thousand causes fever, but remember that the one biting you may just be the bad tick. We start a funny ceremony as we all strip practically naked and, as baboons inspect each other for fleas, we start inspecting each other for ticks!

It becomes even funnier when we suddenly hear human voices approaching. We start dressing fast, while cracking jokes about how baboons would kill themselves laughing at us! Into our sight comes a guide leading an overseas television team making a film in the Drakensberg. After a cordial word we leave them and cross the umpteenth stream to start another ascent.

That day we see two grey rhebok (there are also red mountain rhebok in the area), a duiker and a troupe of baboons. We can also see that there are eland around because of the piles of eland dung, but we don't see even one of the giant mammals. There are also porcupine quills which we pick up in passing. We don't see any cats, such as the serval and the black-backed jackal, although there are hair balls aplenty. According to Dave we should also encounter klipspringers and bushbuck in this area.

Tragedy in Ship's Prow Valley

At lunch-time, with the sun at its strongest, we sit under a few **Cordia caffra** trees in the Ship's Prow River. Two huge crevasses open up in the fork of the Ship's Prow Pass, and lower down they turn into two wide, dry riverbeds strewn with huge boulders. If you look carefully, though, you will see from the soil, grass, branches and even uprooted trees that these dry riverbeds can become seething rivers if it starts raining heavily higher up in the mountains.

This is probably what happened during the first week of January 1981 when a Miss Vorster and two Liebenberg brothers lost their lives here. Nobody knows exactly how they were surprised by the rolling masses of water, and whether it happened during the day or whether they slept in the gorge. Some people even think that there may have been a landslide following the huge storm higher up in the mountains. When the bodies were finally found after a search lasting days, they were badly mutilated as a result of the force of the water and rocks that dragged them along. Dave was on leave at the time, but he collected what was left of their gear — a few pitiful shreds . . .

Had there not been three clearly visible stone cairns on the two banks and in the middle of the Ship's Prow River, we would not have been able to find the path on the other side again.

Interesting beetles

"Hi, everybody! Look! Mom's little beasties!"

We all know that Mom's beasties are dung beetles. Five of them are busily rolling some eland dung.

We call them Mom's beasties because once, when Mom wrote a story for a youth paper, she made a whole study of these interesting little animals. She even wrote to Australia for more information about South African dung beetle eggs which had been exported to Australia in order to counteract their fly plague. The Australian dung beetles only ate kangaroo dung and refused to touch cow dung. The flies could then breed in the cow dung unhindered — until the South African dung beetles, which did not have such scruples, arrived!

"What does the dung beetle do with the ball he makes? Does he eat it?"

"Yes, they are quite clever. They roll these dung balls, bury them, and then later, when there is a food shortage, they eat them. The female rolls the dung ball into

108

the hole, and lays her eggs in it. The layer of soil which sticks to the dung ball as it is rolled along helps to seal it and to keep moisture in. Once the little dung beetles hatch there is plenty of baby food for them to eat. The little ones will only crawl out once it has rained and the soil is nice and soft, and will then instinctively find their own food."

Company on the trail

"There are people over there on the hill," George announces, and starts yodelling. The children are wildly excited when the other people yodel back.

Mom takes off her hat and wipes the sweat off her forehead. "How far have we gone today, Dad? What does the pedometer say?"

The reading is almost 15 kilometres.

"It feels like much, much more!" Mom declares with great conviction.

It is clear that we will have to start looking for a place to camp, as everybody seems to be tiring fast.

We are fortunate because the good weather that we have had the past two days persists. It is not pleasant to be caught in the rain, and then one also travels so much slower.

"There he is!" This is a cry of enchantment from Mias, and we all know what he is referring to because he has been looking out for it for two days now. It is a black eagle, which swoops down and settles, quite unusually, on a low rock. There it waits, probably for prey, such as the dassies which abound on the rocks.

Looking for a camping spot

The majestic panorama changes from moment to

moment. Even though we are tired, the scene remains a feast to the eye. We have now been looking out for likely camping spots for quite a while, and remembering last night's sleep on the uneven ground, we reject every little spot we come across. We have passed the old wire fence and a turnoff to the right. (According to the map this is a shorter route via Van Heyningen's Pass to Injasuti Camp.) If the map is right, there should be another stream just below Sterkhorn (a peak of 2 973 metres, right next to Cathkin Peak). We may as well push on, because finding a level place to camp where there is no water is also useless.

Soon, however, we are rewarded. We find not only the stream, but also a lovely, smooth site next to the contour road. The grass there is soft, so that we have a good prospect of a restful night!

Everybody is overjoyed, because it has been a lovely day, one of the most wonderful yet in the mountains. But it also has been a long haul, as the pedometer shows a clear 20,2 kilometres! Furthermore, it is already five o'clock. At six the sun sets and at seven it will be dark.

Tired and footsore

Mom is so tired that we decide to spare her and to eat bread rolls and carbanossis with salami. If we can each have a cup of instant soup, we will be satisfied. Dad will see to the drinks before we go to bed.

But Dad is also under the weather. His ear is swollen and the gland under the ear has turned into a hard, round swelling. He first noticed the swelling in the morning, and he surmises that a poisonous insect must have bitten his ear. Fortunately our family doctor is also a keen hiker, and he has provided us, as usual, with a broad-spectrum antibiotic.

As usual Dad's heels and big toes are covered in blisters. The expression of disgust on his face disappears, however, when he discovers the can of beer which Marieta digs out of her rucksack — he had forgotten about it!

"Such a pity that your poor old Dad should have such useless feet. Successful hiking depends on two things — your two feet. Feet are a hiker's wheels, except that a hiker does not really have a spare wheel which he can put on when needed . . ." Dad says in great disgust.

"You do become eloquent after only one beer! Turn your foot this way, I want to get the plasters on," Mom says, reminding Dad that she thinks it is all his fault, as he refuses to rub his feet with methylated spirits before going on a hike. "If you take off your boots more often along the route, and rinse them in the mountain streams, you won't get so many blisters."

Barend, who feels that Mom is not displaying enough sympathy at all, takes out his "Made in Hong Kong" pedigree rubber spider and slowly drops the hairy horror in front of Mom's face while she is oblivious to everything but concentrating on her Florence Nightingale act.

You have never seen the likes of it: Mom leaps into the air as if jet-propelled, and spills words she never knew she knew . . .

Dad tries to salvage the situation, but Mom has the bit between her teeth now and she castigates everyone in sight about everything. "Pick up all these chewing gum wrappers! How many times do I have to tell you not to be such pigs!" Yes, Mom is tired. The sun really got to all of us today, but Mom has the most sensitive personality — and tonight it is showing.

The light supper is rounded off with instant pudding

— which, notwithstanding Dad's best efforts, refuses to set. We don't say anything, however. We drink the dessert from our mugs!

In lighter vein

It is quite extraordinary how a simple meal can change a person's mood. Jokes start flying thick and fast. When Dad makes the innocent remark that it is quite dry in the mountains, Barend says that the height of drought is when the fish swim so hard that they create a dust storm. Mias knows better. "The height of a drought is when the trees start running after the dogs . . ."

"And the height of arrogance?" George asks.

This is directed at Mom, but she has to acknowledge defeat.

"That is when somebody who has stolen your fruit knocks at the door and asks for a cloth to wipe his sticky hands!"

A sense of wonder

For evening devotions Dad reads the next two chapters (39 and 40) of the book of Job. In this chapter God tells of the wild goat, deer, ass, ox, horse, hippopotamus and various birds like the ostrich, hawk and eagle.

When at the end of the "natural history" lesson God asks Job whether he would still like to argue with Him, Job's response (40:4) is: "I am unworthy. How can I reply to you? I put my hand over my mouth."

So are we touched by a sense of wonder when we contemplate God's creation.

We sing a verse of Psalm 33 to tie in with this. Instead of saying a prayer, we solemnly sing the last verses of this magnificent hymn.

The moving melody drifts slowly across the moonlit mountain landscape and down the dark gorges . . .

Hiking stories at the end of the day

As usual, this is conversation time. Mom and Dad usually have an interesting topic which they keep for the half an hour before bedtime. The fact that Dad is tamping his pipe, and slowly and with relish lighting it, is a sign that in spite of tiredness he is going to stick to the tradition tonight.

"Dad, are there hiking trails like ours in other countries?" Marieta wants to know.

Dad is willing to provide interesting facts about hiking routes in the USA, England and Europe. He soon realizes, however, that the stories about the hiking history of the Drakensberg which he had told on previous hikes had made much more of an impression. Mom is already dozing in the tent. Marieta has toppled over against her sleeping bag, fast asleep. The other three kids keep their eyes open with the utmost determination.

It is night, high up in the mountains. The night-wind snatches at the tent, and a troupe of baboons not far away seems to be getting restless. Their harsh barking sounds close by in the quiet night. A sudden yah-yah-yahhh! gives me a sudden fright — the jackals have started their nocturnal prowling. It is wonderful to be so close to nature, but the tents are rather insubstantial protection . . . suppose a wild animal should decide to come searching for food here!

4.4 THE THIRD DAY OF THE TRIP

When at half past four I wriggle out of my sleeping bag, I can't believe my eyes — fog has smothered everything in a white blanket as far as the eye can see.

Because I can't see a thing, I crawl right back into my sleeping bag . . .

After breakfast and packing up — which can take quite some time — we are keen to take to the road, perhaps because we know that only two or three hours of hiking remains. All of us slept better than the previous night, and we have reason enough to sing lustily.

It can become very cold in the Berg

Where the road turns off from the contour road to Monks Cowl we come across two hikers who had left from the base camp (Keith's Bush Hut) below Gray's Pass at five that morning. One of the blokes has a huge beard and he looks as if he might have escaped from the illustrated Children's Bible we have at home!

They tell us how cold it was up on Champagne Castle, where they had slept in the snow the night before. The damp which had condensed on the inside of their tent had turned to ice! Their waterbottles outside their tent, and the stream, had frozen up, and they had been so cold that they had practically not slept at all. They had to make coffee every now and then to keep warm, and really started worrying about hypothermia.

"Mom, what does the man mean by hypothermia?" Marieta asks with curiosity.

"That is what happens when your body cools down more rapidly than it can generate heat. Somebody who suffers from this will start shivering, can have difficulty in speaking, finds it hard to walk and can start doing all sorts of abnormal things. If such a person is not helped quickly, he can die."

"What should one do to help?" Marieta asks anxiously.

"The person has to be warmed immediately, he has to be dressed in extra clothing, and must have something warm to drink. He should also be placed in an extra sleeping bag. It will help if somebody gets into the sleeping bag with him to warm him. If he also got wet, he has to be dried off immediately."

"Did you know that all the lovely snow on the mountains can also be very dangerous?"

"No, what can the snow do?"

Dad explains: "The snow can reflect the sun back so strongly that one can be sunburnt. The reflection of the sunlight on the white snow can also cause snow blindness if one is not wearing dark glasses."

"I never knew that!" George observes.

We say goodbye to the ericas and begin to descend, where cheerful little everlastings (helichrysum) bloom in white, yellow, pink and bright red exuberance on the grassy carpet. Lower down, the flame-red bottle brush delights the eye.

Disaster in the mountains

It is Mom who first notices the two boys clambering at speed down the path. When they approach, we can see that they are in distress. They do not have their backpacks with them, and it is clear that they have been running some distance, because they are out of breath when they reach us.

"Why are you in such a hurry? Something wrong?" The two introduce themselves as Graham Carrington and his friend Wynne.

They say that they are on their way to Monks Cowl Campsite to find help. Graham's father had an accident in the Gatberg earlier that morning. He broke his leg above the ankle, and is now unable to move.

Mom offers refreshment which they drink thirstily. They continue their downward run and we also increase our pace. The last hour's walk is completed within half an hour!

When we reach the campsite, Margie is trying without success to raise Dave on the radio. When she finally does reach him, it is to find that he is far from home. He asks her to drive to Kelvin Grove immediately to see whether helicopeter help is available. The Advanced Flying School of the Air Force Base Bloemspruit near Bloemfontein has two annual camps in the Drakensberg, and a camp was in progress at Kelvin Grove.

Dad goes with Margie in the Land-Rover to look for help. We hope for the sake of both Mr Carrington and Dave that the Air Force can help, because getting an injured man down from 12 kilometres up the mountain is no joke — neither for the people who have to carry him, nor for the injured man.

This can happen so easily

While we are waiting, Graham and Wynne tell us the story. They had climbed the Gatberg early that morning. They had almost got back to the Umhlwazine River when the accident happened. Derrick Carrington, the father, was in front, followed by Graham and Wynne. Wynne had stumbled and fallen on top of Graham. Graham, who had not expected this, landed on top of his father, who was of course totally unprepared for this. They all tumbled down in a farcical dominoes style, but when Derrick tried to get up again, he found that he was unable to stand. His leg had broken so badly that the bone ends stuck through the skin!

A helicopter rescue drama

The hammering sound of the approaching helicopter makes all of us run to the landing strip near Dave's house. Soon the Alouette lands. Graham and Wynne explain to Captain Eddie Brown where they had left Mr Carrington, and the helicopter leaves immediately, while we wait anxiously.

Twenty minutes later the characteristic hammering sound is back, and the Alouette lands again. The captain explains that they could not land in the slanting, wooded area, and that they could not see Mr Carrington from the air. The red rucksack which Graham had left with his father was not visible from the air.

Graham would therefore have to come with them to show them exactly where his father was.

Once again the anxious minutes tick away. The news has spread, and apart from Mr Carrington's wife, there are a number of other curious people from the Champagne Castle Hotel.

After another twenty-five minutes the Alouette appears above the trees again. Has he been found this time?

When the helicopter lands, Dave, who has returned in the meantime, runs closer. "Found him?" he yells above the noise of the machine, and runs back to arrange the stretcher and blankets.

Carefully he helps Captain Brown and Sergeants Danie Brink and Mannetjie Wilken to place the injured man on the stretcher. From Derrick's groaning it is clear that he is in intense pain.

When Derrick is finally down on the ground, he tells us how it hurt when he was hoisted to the helicopter with his injured leg strapped to his good leg to stabilize it.

The helicopter returns to the scene of the accident to fetch Graham — he had to remain behind as the helicopter had room only for his father.

Graham is deposited at the forestry station, and Mr Carrington is taken on board again to be flown to Kelvin Grove, where the Air-Force doctor will give him a strong painkiller before transporting him to Estcourt hospital.

So another Drakensberg drama — fortunately not fatal — is added to the annals of the mountains. With a sigh of relief we return to our tents . . .

"Shows you how easily an accident can happen. See why I am always insisting that you should be careful, children?"

It is so late when we have unpacked and showered that Dad decides not to look for a lift to Injasuti Camp to fetch the minibus. That can wait for tomorrow!

Campfire farewell

The sizzle of the sausages and T-bones on the coals is accompanied by music and song. Mias has taken out his guitar and while night enfolds the mountains, we sing one nostalgic song after the other:

"I love to go a-wandering, along the mountain track,
and as I go, I love to sing, my knapsack on my back.
Valderee, Valdera, Valderee,
Valde-ra-la-la-la-la-la, Valderee, Valdera,
My knapsack on my back.
I love to wander by the stream that dances in the sun.
So merrily it calls to me, come join my happy song . . ."

"Dad, don't forget to tell us something about helicopters — you promised." Barend is ready to move on to another topic.

"Later, man. Let us first sing another two farewell songs. Mias will play the guitar for us."

I have forgotten the muscular pains and the tiredness, and join in lustily for **Auld Lang Syne**. I feel a sadness that will stay with me for some time.

I am saying goodbye, but I know I will return . . . again and again . . .

Supper with real meat (not the ersatz of the trail), fresh salad (instead of dried vegetables) and fresh bananas, apples and oranges (instead of dried fruit) is a feast. Being "home" has its benefits!

It was worth it — all the way

When the quiet breathing of the children confirms that they are lost in dreamland, Mom and Dad talk about the past three days.

"Well, we did not get to Champagne Castle, but it was a wonderful experience. Hiking is still the best way to escape the everyday pressures. It gives one a wonderful sense of liberation, and it feels as if we have been away from home for far longer than just five days."

"Yes," Mom agrees. "Without the past three days our lives would really have been the poorer. I feel better, physically and spiritually, and the children also enjoyed it a lot. They learnt a lot; even I learnt a lot."

"One day we must write a book on hiking for the family," Dad muses.

Mom does not even hear — she has succumbed to sleep.

Marieta, Barend, George, Mias, Mom, and Dad say good-bye to all the hiking families and especially those who are still planning to go.

Our goodbye is simply: "Until we meet again" — sometime, somewhere, on a hiking trail in this wonderful country, South Africa.

5. BIBLIOGRAPHY

DOAN, MARLYN. 1979. Starting small in the wilderness. The Sierra Club outdoors guide to families. San Francisco: Sierra Club Books.

DORSEY, JOAN. 1978. Introducing your kids to the outdoors. Boston: Stone Wall Press.

FLETCHER, C. 1975. The new complete walker. New York: Alfred A. Knopf.

LEVY, JAYNEE, 1982. (Fourth edition 1993.) Everyone's guide to training and mountaineering in Southern Africa. Cape Town: C. Struik Publishers.

MANNING, H. 1980. Backpacking. One step at a time. New York: Vintage Books.

OLIVIER, WILLIE & SANDRA. 1989. The guide to backpacking and wilderness trails. Johannesburg: Southern Book Publishers.

SILVERMAN, GOLDIE. 1975. Backpacking with babies and small children. Edmonds: Singpost Books.

SHUTTLESWORTH, DOROTHY. 1978. Exploring nature with your child. New York: Abrahams.

STEYN, A. 1982. Backpack for pleasure. Pretoria: Intergrafix.

STOUT, ANN & JAMES. 1975. Backpacking with small children. New York: Funk & Wagnalls.

PHOTO ALBUM

Peaks and clouds in the Drakensberg

One wrong
step
could be
fatal...

Floral splendour in the
Drakensberg

Climbing higher

Rustic overnight accommodation

On top of Mount Memory

A good place to relax and enjoy the view

Nature's
determination
to survive

Hiking in winter is a
special experience

Floral splendour in the Drakensberg

Sunset on the Inner and Outer Horn, Cathedral Peak

We have made it - together

Looking down on the world

Watching in awe the majesty of Creation

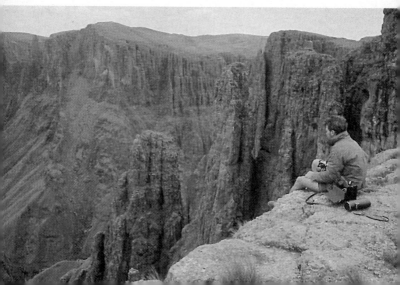

Creatures of the trail

On horseback at the foot of the
mountains

Trying one's luck at the trout waters

A refreshing dip in
a cool berg pool

Different types of gladioli and watsonia
paint the mountain

The view at Vulture's Retreat, Natal Drakensberg

Pressing on, inspired by the
panoramic view

Helicopter rescue of a hiker in trouble

Cooking a warm meal on a cold winter's night

Quenching one's thirst at a clear, clean, cold stream

Breakfast along the way

Ascendng the chain ladder

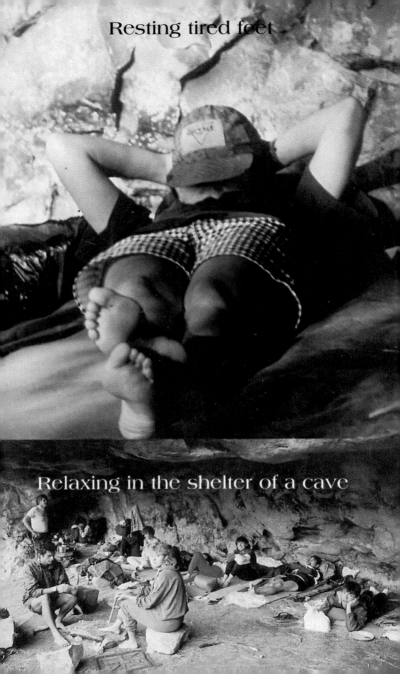

Resting tired feet

Relaxing in the shelter of a cave

Splendour of the Drakensberg

The beautiful
'suicide lily'

Necessities for pleasant hiking: tent with two types of pegs, space blanket, survival bag, mug, water bottle, raincoat, hat, toilet bag, mattress, balaclava, towel and sleeping bag

Cooking and eating utensils

Remember the basic items of a first–aid kid

A variety of hiking shoes and boots are available for men and women

Items to make your trip more enjoyable

The author

A hiking tent for three people

Camping on the escarpment

Tents are available in all shapes and sizes, for camping and backpacking

Marjeanne relaxing in the shade of her tent

The grandeur of a waterfall

Bheki
Khoza,
Natal Par[k]
Board
Officer - i[n]
charge a[t]
Royal Na[tal]
Park,
Bergville[,]
carrying h[is]
baby the
kangaroo[]
style

A mothe[r]
carrying h[er]
baby the
African
(abba) sty[le]

Young Sureta enjoys hiking

Hannetjie (the author's wife), fully equipped for another hiking adventure

Young and energetic Wessel, carrying a heavy pack for a five-day hike

A senior hiker (Willem Postma) taking a break, to enjoy the surrounding scenery.

Bennie van der Walt
on the trail

The Sphinx along the route to Champagne Castle